The Insider's Guide to

RAISING VENTURE CAPITAL

The Insider's Guide to

RAISING VENTURE CAPITAL

Garry Sharp

Foreword by Timothy Waterstone

Endorsed by the British Venture
Capital Association (BVCA)

 KOGAN PAGE

First published in 1991

Kogan Page Limited
120 Pentonville Road
London N1 9JN
© Garry Sharp, 1991

British Library Cataloguing in Publication Data
A CIP record for this book is available from the British Library.
ISBN 0 7494 0283 0

Typeset by BookEns Ltd, Baldock, Herts.
Printed and bound in Great Britain by
Biddles Ltd, Guildford and Kings Lynn

CONTENTS

NOTHING VENTURED, NOTHING GAINED.

It really is extraordinary what you can achieve with the right attitude – and the right support.

Sir Edmund Hillary climbed Everest.

Christopher Burnett bought out the Upholstery Division of Silentnight Holdings, with a £9 million package combining equity, mezzanine and debt.

The information technology recruitment specialists TSI Group, a start-up as recently as 1987, raised their third round of venture funding just two years later, in order to develop their office network.

And no sooner had Morris Bond and his fellow directors completed the complex demerger of the Beck Food Group than they raised £9.8 million in expansion capital to develop the company's manufacturing sites.

Hillary had the support of Sherpa Tenzing Norgay.

The other examples were backed by County NatWest Ventures – one of Britain's largest providers of venture capital, with offices in London, Birmingham, Edinburgh, Leeds and Manchester.

For a forty-page brochure which gives detailed case histories of our achievements, call Helen Walsh on (071) 375 5109.

Or write to County NatWest Ventures Limited, 135 Bishopsgate, London EC2M 3UR.

MANAGEMENT BUY-OUTS & BUY-INS
DEVELOPMENT CAPITAL
EXISTING SHARE PURCHASE

COUNTY NATWEST VENTURES

A MEMBER OF IMRO
& The NatWest Investment Bank Group

This book is dedicated to my mother
and my late father

Foreword

by Timothy Waterstone

'Life for him was an adventure; perilous indeed, but men are not made for safe havens.'

Edith Hamilton on Aeschylus
(The Greek Way)

In all walks of life—political, military, in the Arts, in the Church, in philosophy, in finance, wherever men focus their minds and their lives—there are those who have a compulsion, beyond just a desire, to tear up the pages of perceived wisdom and practice, and to find avenues of innovation and re-direction that stand apart.

John Julius Norwich, in his elegant anthology, quotes, in parallel with Edith Hamilton, Dorothy Parker saying much the same thing about Isadora Duncan: 'There was never a place for her in the ranks of the terrible, slow army of the cautious. She ran ahead, where there were no paths.'

It is perhaps too glib to ascribe to the life of finance and business all the panoply of human experience, and yet it does become for so many of us the central intellectual and functional focal point of our lives. For forty or fifty years we compete, succeed, fail, build dreams, lose dreams, make friendships and enmities, make money, lose money, help some people, manipulate others, work through a complete patchwork of experience and absorption.

Garry Sharp's excellent book, to which I am delighted to contribute this foreword, gives a most clear and concise presentation of the technical considerations that an entrepreneur must master if the new business is to be accurately structured in terms of its financial engineering. And I do emphasise that the entrepreneur must *master* the structure of the capital finance; personally I would never support or recommend support for an entrepreneur who depended wholly on professional advisers—lawyers, accountants, consultants—to write the Business Plan and to negotiate finance.

New businesses will only work if the founder has not only a dream of clarity and perception and genius, but an instinct for money and what it means. You will need the sort of perception which can look down at a situation and see what are the issues which really matter; the wood from the trees, the wheat from the chaff, the connections that will be strung together as the business moves from birth to adolescence to struggling young adulthood to maturity.

The lawyer must not dominate, and the accountant must not dominate. The former is there to protect your rights, and the latter to police for investors.

You—the founder—must have the financial overview and grasp to understand instinctively the way your Business Plan 'works'; the venture's profile in terms of cash usage and cash generation, the criteria you will need to apply against new investment decisions, the relationship between cashflow and profit—you, and not the auditors, should set the accounting standards—and the balance between net marginal contribution on each investment pocket and the central overhead.

The entrepreneur must have the vision of where the company is going as it moves through childhood, adolescence and adulthood. Competitive pressures may change the rules, the national economy may help or hinder, but the entrepreneur must always be looking ahead and holding the vision steady.

I have a horror of companies or charities or any businesses whose management information packs only report on the position as achieved. That is the accountant's view—the score card—and of course it is vital to compare achievement against previous calculations of where the business is going to be at that time point.

But most important is where you are going to from the point you are at, and always the team (the management and the investors together) should have a mutual clarity of understanding about the cash requirements of the business for at least eighteen months ahead at any one time, and its strategic thinking over that period in relation to its marketplace and its competition.

Clarity of vision, and of numeracy, is vital therefore, but needs to be held together by leadership of a very high standard.

I am not certain that leadership is teachable, and it certainly comes in many different forms. It is part clarity of vision, part charm, part rhetoric, part manipulation, part commitment. It is never achieved by bullying, and never held together by fear. Businesses are important things—they should provide security, adventure, self-esteem and the companionship of team-life for those who work in them—and people in their working lives look for leadership and fall apart without it.

A founder of a business is in a uniquely privileged position to give leadership, direction and pride to all those who join the team. They will look to the founder for leadership in all aspects; the business must be confidently secure and competent financially, and the management team must show to everybody a spirit of total commitment and courage.

Anita Roddick wins—and her staff love her—because she shows a sublime clarity in her retail vision, a contempt almost for money, and an apparent inevitability about her success. Nobody is frightened of her, everybody respects her, everybody can understand what she wants.

Clarity, vision, leadership, commitment, courage, grasp. You will need all these, and luck, though the latter will look after itself if the rest is in place. The business will be driven not by greed—making money is a by-product—but by the joy of achievement.

Like Isadora Duncan, the entrepreneur has no place in the slow army of the cautious. The fun is in the running ahead, in the finding of the paths.

Timothy Waterstone
August 1990

Acknowledgements

A book such as this is only as good as the breadth of experience it incorporates, and I owe thanks to the dozens of venture capitalists and entrepreneurs who have, wittingly or otherwise, contributed insight and expertise to these pages.

Particular thanks are due to my friends at Baronsmead, especially Richard Hargreaves and Graham Barnes, for their encouragement and practical support.

Also to Jonathan Thornton, Nick MacNay and Neil Murphy at Close Investment Management for ploughing through the book on behalf of the BVCA; to Timothy Waterstone for his foreword and his copious encouragement; and to James Heneage, Paul Smith and John Watts for some illuminating views from the entrepreneur's side of the table.

Finally, to my wife and daughter, not only for their love and inspiration but for making the writing of this book a financial necessity in the first place!

1

KNOW YOUR TARGET: THE VENTURE CAPITAL INDUSTRY

An introduction

A central element of many of the world's classic games—poker, chess or backgammon for example—is their apparent simplicity. You can learn the rules in a morning, but it takes a lifetime to learn how to play. The venture capital business is much the same. The basic principles of investing in small companies are straightforward and are followed more or less universally; the difference between success and failure lies in their application, both by the company seeking finance and by the investor.

Support from a professional external investor can give your company confidence, status and funding so that you can realise your visions more quickly and profitably than you ever could alone. Venture capital funding will enable your company to accelerate its growth not only by injecting cash and underpinning its balance sheet, but by introducing you and your management team to a range of disciplines, contacts and influences that will stand you in good stead all the way to a public flotation or sale.

But for many companies which have built their plans around support from the venture capital industry, the outcome has been far from satisfactory. Confused objectives, poor communications, inadequate performance, impatience and incompatibility have led to the failure or disillusionment of entrepreneurs and management teams which, with a different type of backing, might well have succeeded.

Raising venture capital is a complex, often confusing and almost invariably frustrating process. Yet your choice of investor and the terms on which the capital is raised will count as a profound and long-term influence on your company's future. The day after you sign an Investment Agreement, pass over a Share Certificate and accept a cheque from an external investor, you wake up to:

- a significant change in the ownership of your company;

- a commitment to follow an agreed strategy and a written business plan;

- a requirement to report on your progress formally, in detail and regularly, to an outside shareholder;

- a series of undertakings which circumscribe your ability to make a range of strategic decisions;

- an undertaking, though never couched as a legal obligation, to provide the investor with the return of his money at a significant premium at some time in the future;

- usually, a new board member with a complex and unfamiliar blend of experience, expectations and responsibilities.

None of these will prove a problem or a hindrance, provided that you have chosen your investor wisely, have agreed the right terms and are able to manage the relationship with your new partner. Nevertheless, the consequences of the series of decisions which the venture capital process entails are so significant that you cannot afford to make mistakes.

This book has been written as a guide not only to the mechanics, rules and details of the fund-raising process, but also to the principles and pressures which drive the investors you choose as your partners. It does not presume to advise on corporate financial management or business strategy and it assumes that you are familiar with basic accounting and financial concepts.

This first chapter is, to return to our games analogy, a summary of the basic rules of venture capital. The remainder of the book follows the chronology of the investment process in depth; it shows you how to play the game.

What is venture capital?

Let's get this clear straight away. By venture capital, we mean the provision of finance to companies or businesses which are not quoted on any stock exchange, where all or a substantial portion of the financier's return arises from his partial ownership of the business or is dependent upon its future profits. In other words, Unquoted Equity: because there is no stock market involved, and because it entails buying a part of a company rather than lending to it. The investor becomes a partner in your business. His success is a function of your success. If you fail, he will have no claim to the return of his investment. If you succeed, he will be entitled to a part of the proceeds.

For the sake of variety, the term 'unquoted equity' will be used interchangeably and synonymously with 'venture capital' throughout the book.

It will help to define a number of other terms at this stage. 'Entrepreneur', 'management team', 'company' and 'business' all refer to you—the party seeking finance. Again, they are used interchangeably in the interests of variety.

An 'investee company' is one that has received funding. Americans use the phrase 'portfolio company', (which we have to admit is less ugly), as it describes an investment which is in the venture capitalist's portfolio.

'Investor', 'venture house' 'venture manager' and 'venture capital executive' all refer to the person, institution or fund management company which analyses and investigates your proposal, negotiates the terms, makes the decisions, invests the money and maintains a relationship with you afterwards. This definition happily confuses individuals and institutions, on the basis that each is a function of the other. Venture capital is a personal business and once in the process of raising finance you are likely to find yourself referring to and remembering different individuals rather than different investment companies.

Finally 'he', of course, also means 'she'.

The scope of venture capital

Our definition of venture capital covers an enormous range of situations, ranging from supporting a next-door neighbour with £5,000 to develop an idea in the garden shed, through to the £2,375 m de-listing and buyout of Gateway in 1989.

Incidentally, it is also a different use of the phrase from the narrower application prevalent in the United States, where venture capital refers solely to investment in young, rapidly growing, often technology related and almost invariably high risk companies. Many people think that the venture capital industry does not take enough risks or support the young companies that it should in this country. This argument is the basis for a fascinating and apparently endless debate to which this book will not contribute; we are concerned with what venture capital is today and how you can use it to grow your business.

The British venture capital industry is large not only in scope, but also in financial terms. During 1989, 1,569 companies raised a total of £1,647 m from the British venture capital industry. This represents an increase of 21 per cent in numbers of companies financed and 60 per cent in nominal money terms on 1987 (source: British Venture Capital Association Report on Investment Activity 1989).

During 1989 alone £1,684 m was committed to the venture capital industry by pension funds, insurance companies and other major financial institutions, confirming its role as an important source of corporate finance into the 1990s (source: UK *Venture Capital Journal,* January 1990). At the end of 1989, the industry had over £6.7 bn under management.

Types of investment

An industry so large in size and scope clearly needs to be broken down into smaller pieces. The first question a venture capital executive will ask, when told about a proposal, is 'What sort of deal is it?' By that, he means is it a Seed Corn, Start Up, Early Stage, Rescue, Expansion, Acquisition, Management Buyout, Management Buyin, Debt Replacement or Replacement Capital proposal? These terms are shorthand to describe the *stage* of the company seeking finance and the *purpose* of the financing.

Seed corn

Our example of investing £5,000 in your next-door neighbour to enable him to develop an idea in his garden shed is a perfect example of seed corn finance. It is an investment aimed at financing the development of a product, often with an imprecise and long-term view of that product's commercial potential.

Start up

The term is self-descriptive. To differentiate it from a seed corn investment, a start up investment must be in a company which

- is ready to start trading immediately,

- has a full management team, or at least most of one,

- has a clearly identified market to attack, and

- has a fully, or nearly fully, developed product or service.

Early stage

Most venture capitalists define an early stage company as one which has
not yet made profits. Some use it to describe a company less than three
years old. However there are some ten-year-old companies which have
yet to make profits, whereas long before its third birthday Compaq in
the US was generating sufficient cash and profits to take over a substantial portion of the entire venture capital industry. The definition is better
based on profitability than age.

Seed corn, start up and early stage investments carry levels of risk for the
investor which set them apart from other types of unquoted investment.
Appraisal of opportunities in these categories is also considerably more
difficult, as there will be little in the way of directly relevant past performance by which to gauge the company's products, its markets or its
management. At some point in the decision-making process, no matter
how much work is invested in research and analysis, the investor has to
act on faith, experience, subjective judgement and instinct.

Investment in companies at these early stages of development probably reflects many people's conception of what venture
capital is.

Excluding rescue capital proposals (to which we shall return later),
the other types of investment entail the financing of established, albeit
often small and fragile, businesses. They are collectively defined as
development capital investments and share a number of features.

1.   The investor can look at an existing, established business and
      management team and, at least to some extent, form a view of
      their likely future performance by looking at their past record.

2.   There will be an existing business of some value, so that the
      investor has the prospect of some return on his investment (or at

least his money back) even if the growth anticipated at the time of investment does not materialise.

3.   An established management team is more likely to be showing any weaknesses or shortcomings already. The venture capitalist can expect to spend less time watching and worrying about the team's performance once he has made his investment.

The British venture capital community has, since the mid 1980s, found development capital proposals more attractive than seed corn, start up or early stage investments. Extrapolation of past performance is an easier basis for analysis than the host of uncertainties presented by a start up. Chapter Four reviews ways in which you can present your case which will accentuate the features which investors find attractive.

Development capital proposals are defined by the use to which the funding is to be put.

Expansion

Approximately 50 per cent of the unquoted equity raised in the UK is used for expansion of an established business. More specifically:

● additional working capital to meet growing trading requirements;

● funding for new product or service development;

● funding for a move into new geographical markets;

● capital expenditure.

Acquisition

We are seeing an increasing tendency for private companies to buy one another, as aggressive and ambitious shareholder/management teams take over from remote family and other absent shareholders. Many entrepreneurs now use private companies, combined with good relations with a group of unquoted equity investors, as vehicles to build significant, diversified groups.

Debt replacement

The combination of sustained high interest rates, falling revenues and high levels of borrowing has turned many private companies with strong historic trading records and profitable performance at the operating level, into loss makers and strained their cashflow. The shareholders of these companies are having to consider the injection of external equity funding in order to address these interest and cashflow problems.

Management buyout

Acquisition of a company by its management team, funded by bank borrowings and, often, an unquoted equity investor.

Management buyin

Acquisition of a company by an outside management team, which will be new to the business.

Rescue capital

Also referred to as turnaround financing, this describes the backing of a management team to turn a loss-making company into profit. It is almost invariably connected with a management buyin, as a new management team is, obviously, a usual prerequisite of a turnaround.

Management buyins, and especially turnaround financings, share some of the features of early stage investments, as the investor does not have the comfort of having seen the management team actually run the company.

Replacement capital

This is simply the transfer of share ownership, where the venture capital investor buys shares from an existing shareholder, without any funds actually going into the company itself. Of course, acquisitions and management buyouts or buyins are also forms of replacement capital, but the term in the context of the unquoted investment industry is normally used to refer to purchase of a minority share in a company from:

Private shareholders. This includes executives of the company, who may wish to sell either because they are leaving or simply in order to raise cash for personal reasons.

Institutional investors. A company may have grown or changed its activities so that it is no longer appropriate for the portfolio of a particular investor. Thus an institution specialising in start ups may, a number of years after investing in a company, sell its shareholding in a now mature business to a specialist in established companies.

Combined types of investment

It is quite common for an investor to be asked to combine two or more types of financing. A management buyout team, for example, may also need equity funding to finance the expansion of their company, or an expansion financing may involve a move into a totally new area and so contain many of the risks of a start up.

Chapter Two reviews the attractions and drawbacks of these various types of investment from the investor's viewpoint.

How the numbers work

The point has already been made that venture capitalists do not expect a fixed return on their investments, but one that varies with the success of the investee company.

It is only by taking a direct share in the business he has backed that the investor can reap a reward large enough to justify the risk he has taken. This leads to the most common complaint about venture capital, as the entrepreneur objects to 'giving away equity'. In fact it is not a case of giving away equity; you sell it, at a price at which both you and the investor expect to benefit.

This does not mean that the investor parts with his cash on some arbitrary terms and hopes for the best; in practice the structuring of unquoted equity investing is an arcane mixture of arithmetic and assumptions. This section explores the basic elements of this alchemy. The subject is discussed in greater detail in Chapter Six.

Capital gain

The investor in unquoted companies expects to sell his shares at some time—in the jargon he will seek to exit, or to realise his investment. The major part of his return usually consists of the profit on this realisation, which generally happens in one of four ways. In decreasing order of importance:

1. The company is sold to another, usually larger company, so that the investor receives cash, some kind of loan notes or publicly quoted shares in exchange for his investment.

2. The company is floated on a public stock market, so that the investor can sell his shares.

3. The investor places his shares privately with another financial institution.

4. The management team or the company buys the investor's shares.

In any case, the investor seeks to make a major capital gain. How does he quantify the gain he expects?

Plunder Limited

Plunder is a fictional management buyout, invented to help us explore the principles and lexicon of unquoted investment structuring. (It could equally be any other type of development capital proposal). The three senior members of its management have agreed with its parent company, Pillage Inc., to buy the fixed assets for their net value of £2.5 m, plus £250,000 for stock at valuation, with the acquisition set to complete on 1 January 1991. The team will also need to raise £100,000 to cover legal, accountancy and fund-raising expenses. The business plan contains the following financial projections:

Year to 31 Dec *£000s*	*1991*	*1992*	*1993*	*1994*
Turnover	4,700	5,640	6,786	8,122
Gross Profit	1,128	1,410	1,692	2,030
Overheads	550	605	666	732
PROFIT BEFORE INTEREST AND TAX	578	805	1,027	1,298
Interest	305	314	255	161
PROFIT BEFORE TAX	273	491	772	1,137
Nominal Tax @ 35%	96	172	270	398
PROFIT AFTER TAX	177	319	502	739

Borrowing

The management team's first step in raising money for the buyout is a visit to the bank, to see how much debt can be raised towards the acquisition cost, in addition to the normal working capital funding. The bank agrees to lend £1.5 m over three years, on the basis that this represents 60 per cent of the value of the assets being acquired and that the interest bill on this could still be comfortably met even if there were a significant shortfall on the sales budget in the first year of trading. An overdraft facility of £1 m is also agreed, in order to finance the £250,000 of stock and future working capital requirements.

NOTE We have glossed over some assumptions here in order to get at the meat of equity structuring. The use of debt will be reviewed in greater detail in Chapter Six.

Equity

This leaves a £1,100,000 gap. The management team can raise £100,000 between themselves by borrowing personally against second mortgages on their houses. They find a venture house willing to put up the additional £1,000,000 of equity required. How much of the company will they require?

By simply taking a pro rata share of their monetary contributions, the split between management and investors would be:

	Amount	*Percentage*
Management	100,000	9%
Investors	1,000,000	91%
	1,100,000	100%

Well, 9 per cent of the company is more than the management has at the moment. But it is not worth the risk associated with the second mortgages they need to take to raise the cash. And there is no 'Sweat Equity' in it for them. Sweat equity (you might hear it called sweet equity by the more decorous venture capital firms) is the extra percentage of the company, over and above that which the management team buy, coming to them by virtue of their importance as its managers.

Fortunately, the venture capital world is competitive enough for investors not to try to get away with terms like those shown above. Instead, the investor will start the investment structuring process by establishing his target return on the investment. The tool most commonly used to measure an investor's return is the Internal Rate of Return, or IRR.

An IRR can crudely be viewed as the rate at which the investor's money grows while it is locked in the investment. (The formal definition of internal rate of return is 'the rate at which a series of cashflows discount to zero'.)

The investor will arrive at his target IRR by considering:

- risk;
- the anticipated duration of the investment;
- the ease with which an exit can be achieved;
- the level of competition for the investment.

Let's assume that having weighed up all the factors in this investment the investor wants his money to grow at 40 per cent a year while it is invested in Plunder. We can also assume that management and investor have agreed that the company will be sold in four years' time.

As the investor's money is going to be locked up for four years, he will want to see his return compounded over that period. In other words, £1,000,000 becomes:

Initial			1,000,000
End of:	Year 1	*plus 40%*	1,400,000
	Year 2	*plus 40%*	1,960,000
	Year 3	*plus 40%*	2,744,000
	Year 4	*plus 40%*	3,842,000

The investor needs to receive 3.8 times his money after four years in order to justify the risk he took in investing it. A straightforward combination of assumptions and arithmetic leads him to see how he might do that.

Exit assumption

The investor forms a view that when he comes to sell in four years' time, the company's exit value (that is, the amount it is sold for) will be a multiple of the After Tax Profits it earned in the year leading up to the sale (the year to December 1994). This multiple is called a Price Earnings Ratio, usually shortened to 'PE Ratio' or 'PER'.

A central, and often somewhat arbitrary, part of the process is the choice of the PE Ratio at which to assume a sale. As a guide, investors usually look at the levels of PE Ratios at which shares in quoted companies in the same industrial sector trade, and apply a discount of 20 to 40 per cent. Clearly, the higher the PE Ratio assumed, the higher the forecast exit value of the company.

Let's assume eight is the PE Ratio the investor lands on, so that at the end of December 1994, four years after the investment, Plunder will be worth:

$$8 \times (\text{Pre-tax Profit to } 31.12.94 - \text{Nominal Tax Charge})$$

$$= 8 \times (\pounds1,137,375 - \pounds398,000) = \pounds5,915,000$$

NOTE We are assuming that in addition to paying this price for the company, the purchaser will also take over the company's borrowings. This is the normal assumption when selling a company on a multiple of profits which have in turn been calculated after deducting interest on those borrowings.

In order to receive £3,842,000 from the sale of Plunder for £5,915,000 the investor needs 65 per cent of the company, leaving the management team with 35 per cent. This could be achieved by issuing Ordinary shares as follows:

£1 Ordinary Shares	Number	Price	Total Cost	% Equity
Management	100,000	£1.00	£100,000	35%
Investors	185,344	£5.40	£1,000,000	65%
TOTALS	285,344		£1,100,000	100%

This shows the effect of 'sweat equity' for the management; in exchange for their personal risk and labours, they are able to buy shares at £1.00 each, compared to the £5.40 paid by the investors. The extra £4.40 over the Nominal Share Price of £1.00 paid by the investors is called a Share Premium.

On the sale of the company at £5,915,000 the management would receive 35 per cent, or £2,073,000. This certainly sounds a healthy return, more than twenty times the team's original investment. But split four ways it comes down to a net profit of £493,000 apiece, or about £295,000 after tax. Not enough to retire on, while for four of their peak working years they have had their houses at risk and settled for lower salaries and older cars than the senior posts they were offered at major public companies would have provided. This is also, probably, the one shot they will have in their lives of achieving a major capital gain. The team will certainly be more enthusiastic if the rewards can be made a little more substantial.

There is also a problem from the investor's point of view. The day after making the investment, it owns 65 per cent of a company worth

£2,500,000. But it is carrying £1,500,000 of debt, which won't be paid off completely for three years. If the company were to be sold soon after the investment (because, say, the management team fell out or the market prospects suddenly worsened), for its fixed asset value of £2,500,000, the first £1,500,000 of the proceeds would go to the bank, leaving £1,000,000 for the investors and management.

Management would do well, receiving 35 per cent of this, or £350,000; an instant profit of £250,000. But the investors would be left with only £650,000; an instant £350,000 loss, when there has been no loss in value in the company itself. The investor would not see all his money back unless the company were sold for over £3,000,000.

It clearly does not make good sense to make an investment which immediately decreases in value by 35 per cent.

The answer to both these problems is to introduce a second type of share.

Preference shares

Having agreed on an equity split between management and investor, there is no reason why the investor should pay more than the management for his Ordinary shares.

So in our example, our starting point would be:

£1 Ordinary Shares	Number	Price	Total Cost	% Equity
Management	100,000	£1.00	£100,000	35%
Investors	185,344	£1.00	£185,344	65%
TOTALS	285,344		£285,344	100%

We now have a shortfall in the financing of £814,656. This is remedied by the investor purchasing 814,656 Preference shares at £1.00 each. We can assume that these shares have no rights whatsoever, except that they have a prior claim over the Ordinary shares on the assets of the company. When the company is sold they are repaid first, and Ordinary shareholders are entitled to whatever is left over after that. The Preference shares are, in effect, simply another way of paying the Share Premium which is necessary to achieve the correct management/investor equity split.

Now look at what happens when the company is sold after four years, for £5,915,000:

SALE PRICE		£5,915,000
Less Preference Shares		£ 814,656
Available to Ordinary Shareholders		£5,100,344
Management	35%	£1,785,120
Investors	65%	£3,315,224
		£5,100,344

This has distorted things slightly; management now gets less than it received under the old structure, while the investor gets a total of £4,129,880 (£814,656 for its Preference shares plus £3,315,224 for its Ordinary shares), which is more than the £3,842,000 needed for the Target IRR of 40 per cent.

This is redressed by amending the equity split again. After some juggling around, we arrive at the following structure:

£1 Ordinary Shares	Number	Price	Total Cost	% Equity
Management	100,000	£1.00	£100,000	41%
Investors	144,000	£1.00	£144,000	59%
TOTALS	244,000		£244,000	100%

£1 Preference Shares				
Investors	856,000	£1.00	£856,000	–

This structure brings us back to the original cash position for management and investors assuming a sale at £5,915,000 after four years. But it is a vast improvement on the other structures we have seen so far.

The first advantage is that, because most of the investor's money is in Preference shares, he is protected should the company sell for less than expected (see table opposite).

This is a great improvement for the investor; his downside is protected as he gets all but £50,000 of his money back if the company is sold for the £2,500,000 it was purchased for. (There is a total loss to Ordinary shareholders of £100,000 in this case—this reflects the £100,000 in legal and professional expenses incurred in doing the MBO.)

		£	£
SALE PRICE		5,915,000*	2,500,000†
Less:			
Bank Debt		–	1,500,000
Preference Shares		856,000	856,000
Available for Ordinary Shareholders		5,059,000	144,000
Management	41%	2,073,000	50,000
Investors	59%	2,986,000	94,000

* Assumes successful sale after four years, on a Price Earnings Ratio basis with takeover of bank debt by purchaser.
† Assumes emergency sale of assets soon after buyout, with bank debt repaid from proceeds.

On the face of it, however, it does not help the management at all. They are no better off on the success scenario, and stand to lose their share of the professional fees on an immediate sale.

This is where the effects of leverage come in. The Preference shares only need to be repaid once, no matter at what price the company is sold. The management has a larger share of the proceeds after this (41 per cent as opposed to the 35 per cent in the original scenario) and so stands to make a more significant profit if it can beat the £5,915,000 target. In other words the value of management's shares is not a constant ratio of the sale price, but increases sharply as the sale price increases. The table below shows the effect of selling the company at various prices (assuming the bank debt is taken on by the purchaser):

| £000s | MANAGEMENT PROCEEDS | |
| | *Original Structure** | *New Structure†* |
SALE PRICE		
2,500	876	674
3,750	1,314	1,186
5,915	2,073	2,073
7,500	2,628	2,723
12,000	4,205	4,567

* Original Structure: Management gets 35 per cent of proceeds.
† New Structure: Management receives 41 per cent of proceeds after repayment of £856,000 in Preference shares.

The benefits to the management team may not, in relative terms, seem enormous, but the use of Preference shares also forms the basis for further structural refinements, which further benefit the management and which we shall review in Chapter Six.

Summary

Unquoted investment structuring today is dominated by the principle that, on the sale of the investee company, the investor gets most of his original investment cost out first, with the profit split with the management as demonstrated above.

If the company is floated on the Stock Exchange instead of sold outright, then the Articles of Association will normally require that the proceeds of a public share sale are applied first to redemption of the Preference shares.

Chapter Six examines investment structuring in detail.

The investment process

The process of raising venture capital can be broken down into a number of stages. Chapters Two, Three and Four review the steps you need to take before approaching a venture capital company. This section is written to give you an overview of the process from the point at which your potential investor first receives a phone call, letter or business plan. We will look at this process in detail in Chapters Five to Nine.

Below is a typical timetable for an investment. It is realistic for a transaction which progresses fairly smoothly. If there is particular time pressure and the investment is more attractive than average, this timescale could be reduced by up to 50 per cent without too much difficulty, but it is more common to find problems which extend the length of the process.

Week	1	2	3	4	5	6	7	8	9	10
Initial appraisal	*	*	*							
Due diligence			*	*	*	*	*			
Negotiation of terms					*	*	*	*		
Syndication/banking					*	*	*			
Formal offer letter								*		
Legal stages								*	*	*
Completion										*

Initial appraisal

This stage incorporates:

- Discussion and summary of the proposal with the introducer.

The venture capitalist will consider:

type of investment;

size of equity requirement;

industry;

track record of management;

current trading performance

in relation to the investment criteria of the fund or funds which he is responsible for investing. Approaching the right investor is crucial.

- Review of the business plan.

If the proposal sounds like a potential fit, the next stage is to read the business plan. The investor is almost certainly not going to want to meet the management team until he has read the plan, unless he is asked to by a particularly respected intermediary and there are good reasons for doing so.

- Meeting with management.

An early meeting or two with management will have two purposes; to form an early view of the team's quality and to ascertain whether their personal objectives allow scope for the venture house to make an investment on attractive terms.

- Internal discussions

No venture capital executive works alone. As soon as he feels he has a runner, he will discuss it in detail with his colleagues. He will normally introduce a colleague to work as a partner on the transaction.

- Informal referral to industry experts

This is only likely to happen at this stage if the venture capitalist happens to know somebody with appropriate specific knowledge.

Due diligence

This is the formal investigation of the proposal. It normally commences once the investor has decided in principle that he likes the proposal and will normally incorporate:

- independent expert's review of the industry, market and business plan;
- technical consultant's report, if appropriate;
- accounting investigation;
- business and personal references.

Chapter Seven looks at this stage of the process in detail.

Negotiation of terms

Practice here varies between different venture capital firms. Most like to agree outline terms reasonably early on, which can be changed as the investigation and due diligence process reveals factors which make the investment more or less attractive.

Syndication and banking

Syndication is the practice of sharing an investment between more than one investor. An investor may wish to bring in syndicate partners:

- because the equity requirement is too large for him alone;

- because the structure requires the investor to have more than 50 per cent of the company (as in our example in the previous section). In this case the investment would be split so that no investor acquired an unwanted subsidiary.

- to avoid an excessive level of exposure to a particular industry or other type of risk;

- to harness the skills or expertise of a different venture house.

It is usual in a syndicated transaction for one investor to act as 'lead', undertaking the appraisal, investigation and negotiation on behalf of itself and all the other investors.

If necessary, the investor will generally also assist with the raising of any debt finance required.

Formal offer letter

This will be provided once the due diligence stage is completed and the venture manager's formal decision-making process has approved the investment. It will set out the terms of the investment in considerable detail and form the basis for the preparation of legal documents.

Legal stages

These are tedious but essential. See Chapter Eight.

Completion

The cheque is handed over and you acquire a new partner. The investor ceases to be a negotiating adversary and, provided you have both got it right, moves round to your side of the table.

Aftercare

Having made the investment, the investor will seek to:

- monitor your progress;
- help where he can;
- work towards a profitable realisation of his investment.

He may come and sit on your board; he will almost certainly reserve the right to join it, and will expect detailed monthly financial and narrative reports.

The investment documentation will require you to seek his permission for certain activities and decisions of a fundamental strategic nature, such as the adoption of annual budgets, major capital expenditure, change in nature of business, acquisition or disposal of subsidiaries and the recruitment of director level personnel.

Chapter Nine looks in greater depth at the long-term relationship with your investor.

The entrepreneurs

As part of the research for this book, three entrepreneurs were interviewed about their experiences with venture capital investors. The three are:

James Heneage, Managing Director, Ottakar's plc

Ottakar's plc is a chain of bookshops, which raised venture capital as a start-up in 1987. In 1989 it raised further equity funding to finance an acquisition.

Ottakar's now owns nine shops located in major county towns throughout the southern UK.

Paul Smith, Chairman and Managing Director, Complete Communications Corporation Ltd

Complete Communications Corporation Ltd is the holding company for a group engaged in the provision of television post production facilities, the production of light entertainment programmes and related activities. It was established in 1981 by Smith, who has raised a total of some £2 m from venture capital investors in three rounds of financing since 1982.

John Watts, Managing Director, Wiltshier plc

Wiltshier plc is, with annual revenues in excess of £200 m, the largest privately owned construction company in the UK. Watts raised £3 m from a syndicate of investors in 1988 to finance the management buyout of the company.

2

ARE YOU READY FOR THIS . . . ?

What the venture capitalist is looking for

It is common knowledge that a very low proportion of the proposals submitted to venture capital houses eventually lead to an investment being made. There are many estimates of the percentage that fail but the typical venture capital company probably invests, on average, in one or two of every hundred applications it receives. This ratio is not as depressing as it sounds, because a significant percentage of the rejections is comprised of the dreamers and con men who pester the industry, but there is no doubt that one of the toughest parts of raising venture capital is getting through the door.

In your first approach to the venture capital industry your task is clearly to sell, and to do it so well that you quickly have a clutch of potential investors competing to become shareholders. This chapter is intended to help with that basic requirement of selling—an understanding of what the buyer wants—by examining the elements of a proposal which make it attractive, or not, to investors. These elements have been broken down into three groups: Management, Growth Prospects and Risk. Each is reviewed individually in this chapter, after which we will look at particular aspects which figure most strongly in different types of investment.

Management

There are some dreadful clichés about the importance of a company's management to an investor. Two of the worst are: 'We don't back ideas, we back managers', and 'The venture capitalist relies on three things when he makes an investment—management, management and management.'

These sorts of aphorisms are not only banal but misleading. There certainly have been examples of an investor backing a team without investigating the commercial details of their proposal, simply because they were good chaps, but they are pretty uncommon and if you know investors with that sort of approach to life you don't need this book.

The reality is that good management teams and good commercial opportunities tend to be found together, and the investor will to some extent use the quality of one to gauge the other. We shall explore in Chapter Seven the methods an investor uses to assess the quality of the management team. First we need to understand the elements he will be looking for.

Entrepreneurial vision

Every enterprise needs an entrepreneur. His is the hardest role to describe, although one of the easiest to recognise. The world of management literature is awash with phrases and sentences which define entrepreneurs and entrepreneurial qualities, and I don't wish to add to them. The venture capitalist will recognise the entrepreneur as the man who, if you stripped him of all his possessions and threw him onto the street, would be washing dishes by the first evening, managing a restaurant in a month, owning one within a year and pioneering a whole new approach to catering within five.

The point is that the entrepreneur has it *within himself* to make money. Being an expert on mass fish farming when the demand for fish doubles, or running a chain of crèches when mothers are being begged to go back to work may make you rich but does not, of itself, make you an entrepreneur. The distinction lies in the difference between luck and judgement.

The entrepreneur is the one who saw those changes coming and positioned himself, his team or his company for them. Most importantly, he could do it again, perhaps in a completely different market.

A venture capitalist backing a team which happens to be able to benefit from a particular combination of external factors is taking the risk that, should those factors change, the team's advantage will disappear. The investor needs to know that the management has the facility to keep ahead of the market and develop ways of taking advantage of changes as it evolves.

Checklist

Can your team demonstrate:

- a clear, objective overall view of your market;

- a thorough understanding of the factors which influence the market;

- the ability to develop strategic visions which provide you with significant competitive advantages;

- the ability to continue the process of original thought and develop your strategy as new opportunities develop and older ones disappear;

- the ability to communicate your understanding of the market and your strategy to an intelligent layman?

Commercial ability

Having the vision is all very well; the investor also needs to see that the team has the business skills necessary to realise this vision at a profit. Sometimes the ability to make money lies within the person who creates the vision; in other businesses, the creative thinker needs to be balanced by a down-to-earth commercial influence.

The venture capital industry's experience with companies built around the exploitation of new technology, for example, makes it particularly sensitive to the need for a team with the ability to make profits early. The enormous potential market which is 'less than three years away' has so often stubbornly remained three years away. The investor these days will want to see its pursuit funded, at least in part, by profits from something today.

We can group a number of attributes within our definition of the ability to make money.

Checklist

Can your team demonstrate an ability to:

- spot specific and immediate market opportunities;

- close sales;

- beat the competition in the marketplace now, as well as in theory in three years' time?

Specific relevant experience

Can your team actually run the business? This sounds like a stupid question and if I were not writing from experience I would not include it. But in practice, a large proportion of applications for venture capital come from management teams who have never previously done what they now propose to do with the investor's money. In the past, some of them have even received funding.

There was for example, a fish processing plant, started up as a greenfield site with venture capital backing. The company's managing director came from the communications industry and although he had a crisp, credible strategic vision of the long-term market for his products, the nearest he had come to handling fish on a large scale was judging angling competitions.

Once the factory was established, the most immediately apparent shortcoming was the management team's lack of ability to sell to supermarkets. After two years of losses, an experienced sales manager was recruited and revenues started to rise to somewhere near breakeven. However the factory staff, horrified by the prospect of actually having to gill and gut fish on a large scale after two years of idleness, all promptly left. This problem too was solved, although not until after the near loss of major supermarket customers due to missed delivery dates, by the recruitment of a factory manager.

The company now began to look as if it might make progress, at which time the other members of that sector of the fish industry, sensing potential competition, withdrew supplies of the company's raw material, live fish, and put it out of business.

The venture capital industry has learnt from its mistakes and if a management team does not have a weight of relevant experience it is unlikely to find backing. Investors will not be prepared to fund a management team's education.

The closer a team's experience to its planned future activities then the better its chances of raising finance. This applies not only in general terms—'I've been in garden gnomes since I was fifteen'— but in specific aspects 'and I know, on first name terms, the fifteen garden centre buyers who will take our first production batch.'

You might not offer this ideal, but the closer you come—or can persuade your potential investors you come—the better.

Checklist

Can your team demonstrate:

- a track record within your target industry or market;

- proven ability to succeed in tasks identical, or very similar, to the ones they will be undertaking;

- specific, detailed market knowledge;

- personal contacts;

- personnel with a high profile in your industry?

Complete skills set

This area is related to the specific relevant experience discussed above. You need to be able to demonstrate that your team offers the range of skills necessary to run the business. The degree and depth of coverage of each functional area that the investor will want to see will vary according to the size of business. Provided that the essential elements— the ability to think strategically and to close sales—are met, he may well be a little more relaxed about some other functions, although attitudes vary between different investors.

We have, for example, backed a management buyout team which did not have a finance director, because we were satisfied that the accounting personnel and systems could produce accurate and timely financial information and because it was clear that hiring a finance director would not prove to be too difficult a task. Actually, it proved impossible, and we are still providing the company's strategic financial guidance. This has certainly had a negative impact on the value of our investment, but it is limited because the Company's core business thinking has been sound and we have been able to cover the financial function.

Incidentally the lack of a good management accounting, forecasting and information system is one of the most common weaknesses of small companies and a recurring headache for the venture capitalist. He is not as close to the company as the executive management team, and is unlikely to know the company's markets. He therefore relies on a constant stream of high quality information, and any shortcomings in this area will act as a strongly adverse influence on his decision. (We shall be exploring in detail information flow to the investor in Chapter Nine.)

Checklist

Can you demonstrate:

- who is responsible for every major function;
- that all members of your team have the necessary experience, training and skills to meet their respective responsibilities;
- that you have established a complete management accounting and information system, which will enable decisions to be undertaken and explained on the basis of objective data as well as the experience and instinct of the executive management?

Internal compatibility

You *must* get this right. And do it before you start talking to investors.

There is no room for taking friendship into account—it is an irrelevance and invariably disappears the first time two friends disagree about a decision which could result in their houses being repossessed.

The only basis for building a team when your personal welfare is at risk is absolute mutual respect and trust. Don't have a sales director whom you expect to overrule, second guess or criticise. Don't team up with a finance director if you suspect the accuracy of his figures, or doubt his understanding of the way your industry operates. Don't have fellow directors in your team who are 'not quite ready' just for the sake of having a particular number of executive directors—bring them in as junior equity partners and make sure your executive board is built of people whom you would absolutely trust to carry on the business in your absence.

Internal compatibility does not necessarily mean that you have to revel in the company of your fellow directors. Many successful companies are formed of people who wouldn't dream of seeing each other socially. (Not that you'll be seeing much of anyone socially for a few years.) It is based on a shared view of the future of the company and mutually compatible personal objectives.

Checklist

- Are individual roles and specific responsibilities clear and well defined?

- Does each member of the team have faith in his colleagues' ability to carry out their roles?

- Do you all share a common vision of the company's future?

- Do you all understand each other's personal objectives?

- Are all the individual objectives reconciled with each other and with the realistic possibilities for the company's future?

Commitment and motivation

This is an area we shall explore at greater length in the next chapter. The investor will be looking at two specific areas:

- Are you committed enough to stay when events don't work out as planned?

- Are your personal objectives going to lead you to build the company in such a way that the investor can expect to realise a cash return on his investment?

Growth prospects

There is a common misconception that 'venture capitalists make high returns by investing in young businesses that grow quickly'.

We have already seen from the 'How the Numbers Work' section of Chapter One that the venture capitalist's return is more than a simple function of the growth rate of the company he has backed. Plunder Ltd was only growing Pre-Interest Profits at an average rate of some 22 per cent pa, while the investor was expecting the value of his investment to grow at 40 per cent a year. This sort of disparity between the company's growth rate and the return on the venture capitalist's investment is common, and results from a combination of:

- buying a company cheaply (ie at a low Price Earnings Ratio) and selling it more expensively (high PER);

- leveraging the investment with bank debt, which gets repaid before the company is sold or floated.

It is quite feasible to invest in a company which produces a flat profit performance for three years but, provided it has sufficient cashflow to repay heavy levels of debt, achieve a quite healthy return for the investors.

So when we refer to growth prospects we might not necessarily mean the growth of the company itself. The investor may also see the value of his investment grow by virtue of financial engineering which is built around the cashflow generated by his investment, and by external changes which mean he can sell his investment on a higher valuation basis than that on which he purchased it.

There is a full chapter (Chapter Six) of this book devoted to financial engineering techniques which enable an investor to turn an apparently boring investment into one which offers the potential of significant financial return. In this section, we will look at the potential growth of the investee company itself from the investor's viewpoint.

For the investor, there is generally only one measure of corporate growth, and that is profits. Watch any venture capital executive when you show him a set of financial projections and the odds are his eyes will go to the profit line first, to get a quick fix on the anticipated level of growth—then he will go back and work down from the turnover line to see if it makes sense. Large increases in turnover every year are certainly not a prerequisite and forecasts built around exponential growth sales are in for a rough ride from any analyst.

Strategies for growth

Growth plans will be built around a clear strategic vision of the market and the company's role in it. The most attractive proposition for a venture capitalist is one which summarises this strategic vision in clear terms which can be understood by a lay investor and validated by independent market research.

A good example is the transportation company which has identified an opportunity (it is too significant to be called a niche) in the retail distribution market. It specialises in distributing to the large DIY retail stores. The DIY chains do not have central distribution facilities and there is no wholesaling industry to serve them, so suppliers have to deliver direct to each store. For many smaller suppliers this is a nightmare, as the cost of buying space on parcel lorries destroys their profit margins. But the company achieves significant economies of scale by taking goods from many different suppliers into a centralised warehouse and then running full trucks to each store.

There is a good example of a clear and easily understood strategic vision. Its validity is not difficult to check out by talking to independent industry sources, while a view on growth prospects can be formed by looking at the structure of the industry which supplies DIY retailers and researching and forming a view on the future of DIY retailing as a whole.

A more difficult one is another company, which makes accelerator boards for networked personal computers. The company's resident electronic genius has developed a range of electronic boards which enable computers to talk to each other a couple of orders of magnitude more quickly than they do otherwise. This, on the face of it, was an attractive investment. The company had gone straight into profit, all the major computer distributors carried its products and it needed funding to develop the next range which would work even faster.

But how does the investor form a view on the company's long term strategy? The market is critically dependent on technological developments completely outside its control. And to form a view of what these are likely to be, the investor has to understand both the technology and its application by dominant potential competitors. It's easy to ask 'Why doesn't IBM do this itself?'—understanding the answer is likely to be more difficult.

The above paragraphs are intended not as comments on the relative validity of the proposals or strategies—this is not a book about management or corporate strategy—but simply to illustrate that for the investor, some strategies and markets are easier to understand and to analyse than others.

No matter how complex your market, and how convoluted and intricate your strategic plans have to be, work hard at reducing them to a short summary which an intelligent, commercially minded layman can empathise with. We shall return to the theme of communicating with potential investors in Chapters Four and Five.

Checklist

- Do you have a clear strategy built around your view of the market and its direction?

- Can you explain your strategy and your perception of the market to an intelligent outsider?

- Is your strategic plan clearly reflected in the way the company is structured and operated?

Your market

Some markets grow extremely quickly and offer enormous potential for profit. Like skateboards. The point is that to be suitable for a venture capital backed company, they have to be long-term markets. After all, the investor makes his profit when the company is sold or floated. You can't sell shares in a company which has just gone ex-growth.

So the most important market criterion from the investor's viewpoint is longevity. He has to be able to see that your company's markets are likely to sustain growth over a long time period.

A significant related factor is stability. Although instability in a market may appear attractive in that it offers potential for new entrants, it may discourage a potential investor. Highly unstable markets are difficult to understand and analyse. In addition, venture capital backed companies do not have spare financial resources, so that the financial consequences of an unexpected, significant change in market conditions can be disastrous.

Checklist

- Is your market likely to grow over a long period?

- Are you in a stable market?

Risk

I joined the venture capital industry from an American bank, where I specialised in lending to small, rapidly growing companies with large capital expenditure requirements. In other words, I thought I knew a thing or two about risk. So, the first venture capital Investment Committee I attended was something of a shock, when a full thirty minutes was spent cataloguing the apparently enormous range of things that could go wrong with the investment proposal under discussion. After apparently agreeing that any terrestrial event up to and including the reappearance of the Plague would damage this company, the decision was taken to invest.

The point is that every unquoted investor takes significant risks and stands a very real chance of losing all his money. If you meet a venture capitalist who has never had an investment wiped out, then you've got the junior; insist on dealing with his boss. The professional investor does, however, make it his task to understand every aspect of the risk he is taking when he makes an investment. Losing money because something, which he thought might happen, does happen, is acceptable; getting wiped out by a development he never saw coming is failure for a venture capitalist.

All this is not intended to imply that all investors are supermen who can play twenty moves ahead in the commercial chess game, but simply that they will not invest until they feel they have fully understood all of the risks involved and those risks have been minimised as far as possible.

You can make the investor's life easier—and so increase the chances of getting his backing—by being totally open and frank about your perception of the risk areas you face. Don't leave him to try to work them out by himself.

We can break risk down into four main areas, which are reviewed here in descending order of importance (importance is defined as how often they seem to cause trouble to venture backed companies).

Management risk

The risk that the management team will fail to perform. The most common causes are:

●   Lack of intimate market understanding.

The company is unable to sense and anticipate changes in its markets.

The marketplace in reality is often vastly different from the ordered rationality implied in the business plan. Making analytical sense out of apparent chaos, distinguishing the underlying trends from the actions of specific personalities and relating day-to-day events to the longer-term influences on an industry is virtually impossible without a deep and detailed understanding of your markets and the personalities that dominate them.

●   Inability to renew entrepreneurial vision.

The company is unable to evolve its strategies to keep pace with changing external factors.

A business will not survive for long enough to provide investors with a reward if it does not renew the creative thinking that lay behind its original business plan. The venture capitalist does not know how or when the management will need to renew its creative thinking; he is taking the risk that they will not recognise the need or will lack the creativity to do so.

●   Unfamiliarity with the industry.

Absence of the hands-on knowledge and contacts necessary to do business.

A major problem for venture investors has been management teams' inability to put their plans into practice, because they are unfamiliar with the nuts and bolts of the industry. It is no good having a brilliant long-term plan to penetrate the market for car wiring looms if you are ignorant of the fact that the industry's major players are locked into long-term co-development programmes with fibre optic cable manufacturers.

●   Specific management incompetence.

The inability of the team, or a member of the team, to perform their primary functions.

This comes a little way down the list because the venture capital industry is now fairly experienced at assessing functional competence. Nevertheless mistakes are made and it remains a significant risk area. Chapter Seven looks at how you can expect the investor to form a view on your team's competence.

- Internal incompatibility.

The management team fall out with each other.

This tends to happen when the company is under pressure, because the pressure itself magnifies any weaknesses in the team's internal structure and relationships. Of course, this guarantees that things will go awry at the worst possible time. The investor will seek to minimise the risk by ensuring that the team members are all individually competent and share compatible objectives.

There is always something unpredictable; two of the most catastrophic and expensive fallings-out I have seen were triggered by members of the management team sleeping where they oughtn't.

Product risk

The risk that the product does not work, or that the service cannot be delivered. The definition can be extended to include:

- difficulty in producing goods or delivering services on an increasing scale;

- difficulty in developing further versions to keep pace with market change.

The expertise of the venture capital executive is, clearly, likely to be limited in these areas. Unless your company is very well established or providing a basic and straightforward service, expect him to appoint an industrial consultant who will review the technical aspects of your operation.

Market risk (or External risk)

Broadly, the risk that developments in the market, outside the company's control, will not take place as anticipated. The venture capitalist will attempt to minimise this by undertaking extensive independent market research, and backing management teams who know their markets well. The specific aspects of market risk are as follows:

- Potential market fails to emerge.

This was a major problem faced by investors in the early and mid-80s, when the venture capital industry devoted much of its attention to backing technology related start-ups and early stage companies.

A great number of business plans seemed to have followed a formula. The potential size of the market was calculated based on some extremely conservative assumptions and then divided by a factor of three or four to be even more conservative. Financial forecasts showed that the company in question only needed a tiny percentage of the market to make enough money for everybody to retire.

This often did not work in practice. The reality usually turned out to be that the market was about five times as big as the business plan expected, but took three to five years longer to emerge (by which time the young venture backed business had run out of cash) and came to be dominated by one giant company or a number of them.

Most venture capital executives have been through a number of such experiences and are scarred by them—don't expect a warm reception for a business plan based solely on a global premise about an emerging market.

●   Market shifts away from company's specific product or service.

This can be expected to happen to companies whose strategies are based solely on the extrapolation of past activities. Markets are dynamic and this again reinforces the need for a management team to incorporate a streak of creative strategic thought.

●   Competition.

It is common for a management team, while raising money, to fail to admit to the investor the true strength of the competition. I wonder whether some management teams have admitted it to themselves.

Be prepared to give your investor a full breakdown on your competitors' true market position and their strengths as well as their faults. While you may think you have developed a sound explanation of why every other player in your industry is fatally flawed, the venture capital executive will undertake his own investigation and a different set of answers will destroy your credibility.

Financial risk

By financial risk we mean the assortment of risks presented by the company's funding structure and external events over which it has no control. Running out of cash because sales have fallen far short of budget is not a financial risk of itself—running out of cash because sales are slightly short of budget and interest rates have risen reveals a weakness in the funding structure and is a financial risk.

A full chapter (Chapter Six) of this book is devoted to financing structures and will explore this area in greater depth.

Types of investment

In the first chapter we categorised different types of investment, by using a combination of the *stage* of the Company receiving financing and the *purpose* of the financing. All investment opportunities within a certain type will share a number of common features, irrespective of the fact that they may be in different industries.

This section takes each type of investment and identifies the elements which will be foremost in the investor's mind when he analyses it.

Start-ups and early stage investments

What do investors find attractive about start-ups? The frank answer from many will be 'nothing much'; so far the UK venture capital industry would, on balance, be richer if it had never backed any start-ups at all, such has been the level of failures. Over the last two years or so it has become exceptionally difficult to raise finance for start-ups, reflecting the industry's reaction to the losses it made during the early and mid-80s.

However there are signs that the trend may be in the first stages of a reversal, due to three factors. The first is that venture capitalists have built up a mass of expertise in the techniques of financing start-ups. This can be expected to improve the quality of investments, and there is a growing feeling that this expertise should be put to use. At the same time, losses in some of the buyout and development capital funds have demonstrated that investing in established companies is not the low risk sinecure it may have appeared. The final reason is the sheer weight of money in the industry for which the venture fund managers must find a home.

Start-ups and early stage investments do have a single major attraction; they can prove extremely rewarding for the investor when they work. This is because:

- by definition, successful start-up companies can grow very quickly;

- the investor can expect to negotiate terms from a position of strength, as often he will not be competing with other sources of finance.

You can expect the potential investor in a start-up to pay special attention to the following areas.

Management

The investor in a start-up is dependent upon the performance of management to a greater extent than in any other proposal. An established company will have some inherent value and some sort of momentum in its trading, so that if management fails to perform or loses interest there is at least the prospect of selling it or attracting new management. A start-up, on the other hand, is nothing but the management, their vision and ability.

The factors which will attract special attention will be the team's commercial ability and specific relevant experience, because the pressure on a start-up is to get into profit and positive cashflow as soon as possible, and to get as much right the first time as possible.

The most attractive management team for a start-up is one which is experienced and has a high profile in its target industry, and wishes to start a company because it has identified a better way of doing things.

Because the company itself has no track record, the venture capital executive will research the executives' backgrounds and skills in great depth.

The next most important area for the investor will be entrepreneurial vision. Clearly the strategy has to be right (this will be covered when the investor looks at growth prospects) but at this stage the investor will be more concerned with ensuring that the team can roll their sleeves up and make profits, rather than speculating on, say, the likely state of non-magnetic mass storage media in a decade's time.

So far as compatibility and motivation are concerned, the team will have demonstrated their commitment and mutual trust by leaving secure jobs and taking second mortgages to start a business from scratch. The investor will probably be more relaxed about these aspects than he will be with an opportunistic type of financing such as a management buyout.

Finally, a complete skills set will not be available; the investor will simply wish to reassure himself that it can be built up as the company grows.

Growth prospects

Growth in a start-up is generally predicated on the success of some new approach to a market or industry, which will be built on a series of strategic assumptions. The investor will spend a great deal of time assessing the validity of the approach and the strategic assumptions behind it.

One of the reasons cited for the disappointing performance of start-up funds in the UK is the small size of this country's market. This prohibits those companies which are successful from becoming large enough to provide an investor with the size of return he needs to balance the large number of failures a portfolio of start-ups will contain. The opening of Europe as a single market may enable these companies to grow larger without facing all of the risks and pitfalls which accompany a move into overseas markets.

In any event, the investor will be attracted by a start-up which has the potential to become large enough to provide an enormous return. The pattern of many successful start-up portfolios in the United States is of one, two or three investments providing returns of twenty, thirty or even a hundred times, making up for the outright loss of the other thirty or so investments.

Risk

Every type of risk is present in abundance in a start-up, and there is a limit to what can be done to minimise them. The investor will take the high level of risk as the basis for his negotiations on the terms of his investment.

Expansion finance

More than a half of venture capital investments are expansion financings for established companies. This business forms the bread and butter of the industry and all of the elements of analysis outlined in this chapter will apply to varying degrees.

The investor's job is made a great deal easier by the existence of a track record, and to some extent he can extrapolate from the past, rather than having to make the leap of faith required to invest in a company which has yet to establish itself.

Management buyouts and replacement capital

These investments became extremely popular in the venture capital industry during the mid and late '80s, primarily because they seemed so easy. A simple change of ownership of an established, profitable business with a complete management team. Easy to analyse because everything is in place.

However the dream has turned a little sour recently. The major reason for the well-publicised problems of the major retailing buyouts has been the over-aggressive financial engineering that was required to pay high acquisition prices, loading companies up with excessive debt so that they were unable to cope with the combination of a downturn in their markets and sustained high interest rates.

Apart from the requirement for a realistic purchase price and financing structure (see Chapter Six), the investor will bear a number of other points in mind:

●   Entrepreneurial vision

Does the man who has for the last five years run an obscure subsidiary of a major conglomerate have the creativity and drive to lead an independent company in a developing market? Where did the entrepreneurial flair come from while it was part of a group?

●   Internal compatibility and commitment

Management buyouts are generally opportunistic. For many middle-of-the-road industrial managers, they come along once in a lifetime and represent a single opportunity to amass a large amount of capital. A management team is liable to go to quite considerable lengths to raise the funding it needs, and if this means covering over some deep personal chasms within the team, then so be it. These can lead to problems later if and when trading becomes difficult.

The investor will therefore pay particular attention to making sure that the team will remain together and is not simply on a 'money for nothing' ride.

Management buyins

Management buyins have attracted increasing attention over recent years from the venture capital industry. These transactions are often compared to buyouts, as they entail the acquisition of a complete, existing business from its parent or (occasionally) holders of its quoted shares. However there are some fundamental differences, which revolve around the fact that a buyin incorporates a new, incoming management team. The first weeks after a buyin is completed are a fraught time, as management and investors discover whether what they expected to buy is what they have in fact bought, whether the business can be run as assumed in the plan and, from the investor's point of view, whether the management team can do with the business the things it claimed.

The investor in a buyin faces a compounded uncertainty; the management team will not know the target in intimate detail, and in turn the investor will probably not have been able to see the team in action.

Finally, there is implicit in most buyins an element of turnaround, or at least a claim by the incoming management that they can exceed the performance of the existing team. The requirement to achieve this improved performance adds another layer of risk and uncertainty for the investor.

3

... AND IS IT WHAT YOU WANT?

Should you be raising venture capital?

'I wonder whether people have to ask themselves what they expect out of the company when they start the company up. How many people . . . sit down and say "now precisely what am I attempting to achieve here? What is it I want to do? Do I want to be a millionaire? Do I just want to satisfy my creative urges or to prove my entrepreneurial flair or whatever?" '

Paul Smith

'I believed that venture capitalists were usurers, demanding outrageous rates of return. We did have some funny ideas about venture capital . . . we thought it was spivvish.'

John Watts

The role of venture capital

As we saw in Chapter One, the unquoted investment industry has grown enormously, in both size and scope, during the 1980s. It is worthwhile noting the extent of corporate financing requirements which can be met by the industry.

At one end of the scale, the role of seed corn finance is evolving rapidly. A number of specialist seed corn investors are open for business and, although many would claim that there are too few for the country's needs, at least this specialist discipline is established and growing. During 1990 the BVCA led a number of initiatives aimed at promoting the growth of seed corn investing, reflecting the industry's acceptance of the sector's growing importance.

Start-ups and early stage companies have waned in the industry's favours since the mid-80s, due to their generally poor performance. However there are clear signs that the nadir is past. During 1989, 521 investments, totalling £215 m, were made in start-ups compared with 384 investments totalling £130 m in 1988 (and 1988 itself had shown nearly 20 per cent more financings in this category than 1987). In

February 1990 3i plc, the largest venture capital group in the UK, announced that it had doubled its pool of funds available for start-ups to £100 m. Expect the growth in start-up and early stage financings to continue, for the reasons we identified in Chapter Two.

At the other extreme, unquoted equity investors are beginning to make significant inroads into the role of the quoted equity markets, particularly the Unlisted Securities Market. Investments in excess of £25 m, primarily for buyouts but increasingly for expansion financing and buyins, are commonplace. The quoted equity markets have disappointed many members of the corporate sector with short-term views, lack of fundamental understanding of the companies whose shares they own, susceptibility to extraneous influences and a lack of the liquidity which is, after all, their *raison d'être*.

It is now perfectly feasible for a company to raise in excess of £50 m for an acquisition or expansion programme from the venture capital industry. This approach offers a number of advantages over the use of quoted paper:

● Straightforward process

For a large, established company to raise unquoted equity finance requires it to deal with a handful of investment executives, who are qualified and prepared to investigate the proposal at length and appraise it on its fundamentals, with limited regard to current external equity market conditions.

The process is significantly cheaper and less regulated than achieving a public quotation.

● Investors' patience

The venture capital industry invests with the expectation of realising a profit in years rather than months. Unquoted investors do not expect to dispose of shares in response to short-term performance or market fluctuations.

● Consistent share price

The share price of an unquoted company is only adjusted when new shares are issued, existing shares change hands or the company encounters problems which significantly reduce its value.

● Adequate liquidity

Unquoted shares can of course be bought and sold, although they rarely are because the institutions holding them are geared to long-term investing. This may change, as, for example, investors specialising in nurturing young businesses sell on their holdings in companies which have now reached more maturity to investors seeking lower risk and a steady dividend income. Incidentally, it is not uncommon for executives of established, unquoted companies to sell small portions of their personal holdings from time to time to institutions, in order to unlock some personal wealth as their value grows.

- Simple communications

The process by which investors in unquoted shares keep track of their portfolios—described in Chapter Nine—is, in the main, constructive and informed, and investors' decisions are driven by the company's performance and requirements, not external market conditions. Communications with investors are not hampered by the insider trading rules and other Stock Exchange regulations which govern the quoted markets.

Appendix I contains a case study of £10.6 m raised for an acquisition in less than a week. The management team subsequently raised a further £6 m from the unquoted sector for an additional acquisition, in a private placing organised within six weeks.

The upshot of all this is that if you are seeking financing between £100,000 and £2 bn (£2 bn being the size of the acquisition of the Gateway supermarket chain in 1989, financed by venture capital investors), then some part of the venture capital industry will be geared to meet your needs. This does not, however, mean that venture capital is necessarily the most appropriate source of finance for your company. This chapter invites you to take a look at your motives for raising unquoted equity and indirectly, because they are inextricably linked, some of your motives for running a business.

Ownership and the entrepreneur

The proprietorial instinct is an integral part of an entrepreneur's drive. Without an element of ownership, two of his major objectives—the need to build something of his own vision, and the prospect of a substantial financial gain—cannot be attained.

One of the functions of venture capital is to provide the entrepreneur with the means to realise his visions and become wealthy without diminishing the extent or the strength of his motivation. Nevertheless, selling equity to a professional investor is bound to result, to some extent, in the dilution of the management's ownership and the acceptance of a degree of outside influence and authority.

You need to consider carefully whether this will seriously influence you and your team's performance and motivation. The questions below may be helpful.

Do you feel the need to own a business before you can give it the dedication that exceptional performance requires? And what does the concept of ownership mean to you? To feel a sufficient level of ownership in order to motivate you, do you need:

- a 100 per cent equity interest;

- a majority equity interest;

- leadership of or control over a group of shareholders which collectively accounts for a majority equity interest;

- the largest single equity interest;

- a significant minority interest;

- enough equity to hold out the prospect of becoming seriously wealthy from the company's success?

Or alternatively, do you need:

- to have close day-to-day control over the company;

- to make all major strategic decisions;

- to lead or significantly influence a group which makes the key decisions?

There is no right or wrong in any of the above (except that if you are hell-bent on retaining a 100 per cent equity interest in your company then venture capital is clearly inappropriate as a source of finance). The important point is that before entering into negotiations with potential investors, you have to consider how the presence of outside shareholders and a new strategic influence will affect the way in which you are motivated. The combination of a dilution of a management team's shareholding and the boost (if only temporary) to its cash position which arises on taking an outside investor has been known to make the team lose its edge.

We can illustrate the effect of venture capital finance on management motivation with an extreme example. There was during the mid to late 80s a rash of investments described as 'proactive' deals, where a venture capitalist with strong knowledge of a particular industry or technology would spot a market opportunity and establish and fund a company to exploit it, finding a management team which received a portion of the company's equity in the usual way. The problem was that this team often felt no sense of ownership—it was as if they had been hired by a division of an anonymous corporation and given some stock options as part of the package. Every month, when the company failed to hit its product development or sales targets, the team would merely turn around and say to the investor 'well, we did our best', as if the investor was an employer.

Your personality

James Heneage of Ottakar's plc remarked that the kind of personality an entrepreneur needs to start up a company makes him 'congenitally unsuitable to . . . manage other people's cash'.

His point is that the obsessive, single-minded drive required to turn an idea into reality conflicts with the balanced, rational, profit-focused professional management that venture capitalists like to back. The theoretical answer to this conflict is to team the visionary genius with a commercially astute manager and so get the best of both worlds. (This does beg the question whether the founder of the business is willing to allow his creation to be sullied by petty considerations such as cash and short-term profit.)

Before raising venture capital, make sure that you have thought about the effect the new range of influences and demands on your business will have on you personally.

As a successful entrepreneur, you will think about and have a view of the future. You probably have a vision, a model of where you hope to be in three or five years' time. Amend it to incorporate an external investor. Think through the terms on which you anticipate raising finance, and the nature of the relationship you expect to have with an investor.

The chairman of a company which has recently received venture capital funding remarked of its managing director 'In his head, he understands the need for the controls and influences the investor wants, but in his heart he cannot reconcile himself to sharing his authority'.

For this to work, you must be comfortable, both rationally and emotionally, with the model of your company with an outside investor.

Reasons for choosing venture capital

Bad reasons

- It's cheaper than bank financing.

Equity finance certainly does look cheaper on your Profit and Loss Account, with perhaps a 7.5 or 10 per cent dividend on the Preference shares, sitting below the profit line, instead of an interest charge in your overheads. But in reality venture capital is one of the most expensive forms of financing available, with investors seeking a return of more—often considerably more—than 30 per cent pa. The difference is that this return is taken not from the company itself but from the other shareholders, whose interests are diluted by the selling of shares to the investor and whose entitlement to a dividend takes second place to the investor's.

Of course the company only exists to provide a financial return to its shareholders, so that any form of financing which, as a means of strengthening the company, ultimately reduces the return to shareholders is potentially self-defeating.

- We need the strategic input of an outside investor.

Venture capitalists often do play a role in the strategic direction of a company, and the majority of venture backed companies acknowledge the extent of the practical help they receive. But the interests of an investor will be primarily to protect his investment and secondly to earn the maximum return from it. Most of the time, because he is a shareholder, these interests and those of the company's management and its other shareholders will be identical.

But not always. For example, you may wish to pursue a major acquisition or expansion programme which puts the entire company at risk. The potential rewards for you as a shareholder are enormous, while all you risk is your comparatively small personal investment and a job. It is quite conceivable that should you fail, the presence and prestige in your industry created by your initiative will benefit you personally so that the risk in professional terms is very low. The investor, for whom the financial rewards of success will not be proportionately so great, faces the risk of losing his entire investment with no compensating rewards whatsoever. Conflicts such as this arise with every investment and are bound to distort the input you receive from your investor.

A further problem with relying on strategic input from an investor is your lack of control over the quality of that input. Even if you manage to find a venture capitalist prepared to finance you on acceptable terms, whose advice you value, there is no guarantee that he will always be able to devote sufficient time to you, retain responsibility for his venture house's investment in you or even stay with the house.

If your board needs strengthening with a non-executive director, choose and employ one directly, whose loyalty will be directly to you, rather than indirectly through his responsibility for an investment. By all means use and benefit from the support provided by an investor's non-executive, but do not build your company's future around it. The exception may be for a company raising seed corn or start-up financing, where an executive of the investor is contracted to fill a specific gap in the management team.

Some good reasons

- Your proposal presents too high a risk to be funded by any other means.

- Your company needs to strengthen its equity base in order to expand.

The essential point is that the venture capital investment must earn its return, by taking risks and allowing you to achieve objectives which would otherwise be beyond your reach. It is only on these terms that you should be prepared to accept dilution of the existing shareholders' interests.

Alternatives to venture capital

Make sure you have considered them all. Here is a checklist.

Private investors

The Capital Transfer Tax and its ancestors have, over the last few decades, had a profound effect on the way small companies are financed, as the 'Aunt Agatha' route has all but disappeared. Nevertheless, wealthy individuals do sometimes back young ventures and are particularly common where the amount required is less than £200,000 or so. The advantages are:

- a simplified (or absent) due diligence and documentation process.

- often, more favourable terms than those which would be extracted by a professional investor. (Not always. I remember once spending a week working on an investment proposal, only to discover that the company seeking funding had a private investor lined up and pretended to need equity finance from us only in order to learn what kind of shares to issue).

- sometimes, an investor who takes a personal interest, rather than a salaried employee of a large investment institution.

But watch out for:

- Confused objectives on the investor's part, which can cause serious problems. Ensure that your investor knows exactly why he is investing, and understands how and when his return might come. You do not want equity provided in a fit of enthusiasm by an investor who has not thought through the longer-term consequences.

- Meddling. The professional may take a board seat but will not expect to interfere with the running of your business. An individual with time on his hands may feel his £100,000 investment gives him the right to treat your company as his plaything.

- Sudden need for exit. A change in your investor's personal financial position could lead him to ask for his money back. If you feel morally—or are legally—obliged to meet this request the consequences can be disastrous.

- Depth of pocket. The early stage company financed by private investors will generally require further equity funding as it grows. Individuals are often unable to provide this—the inability of private investors to subscribe further rounds is a major shortcoming of BES financing—so that the company either fails or raises equity from the venture capital industry.

Ensure that you won't be embarrassed by a private investor's inability to support you at a crucial moment. Also ensure that your private investors are prepared to accept dilution of their holdings at a later stage if you raise further equity externally.

All of these points can be addressed. Provided that they are, having a private uncle can be a very satisfactory way of financing your early growth. If you are lucky enough to know an individual who is keen to finance you, then use this book as a guide to putting the investment on a professional footing and you can have the best of both worlds.

Factoring

Sometimes an answer to overtrading. However you need high quality, prompt paying debtors and clean invoices. A bad—or even late—debt of any size can destroy a company whose gearing is disguised by a high level of invoice factoring.

Most banks now offer overdraft facilities, such as the Tandem arrangement operated by Barclays, which emulate a factoring facility by providing an overdraft facility linked to a specific, (and usually high) percentage of high quality current debtors, with less emphasis on your balance sheet.

Invoice discounting, which is often linked to credit insurance, is growing in importance as a means of financing debtor growth.

Medium or long-term debt

Chapter Six incorporates some views on the levels of debt a young, growing company should accept. There is a great deal of competition among banks in the UK corporate lending sector, so that companies are sometimes offered greater facilities than sound financial planning would suggest. Make sure that you, not a bank employee, decide the appropriate level of debt for your company.

A corporate partner

Chapter Ten reviews corporate venturing.

Project financing

If you are planning to raise equity to finance a specific project which is a discrete addition to your business rather than an integral part of it, consider the possibility of funding it as a separate entity outside your core business. For example, a US company setting up a European distribution operation established it as a start-up company in the UK and raised local equity finance, without directly diluting the equity in the core company or affecting its balance sheet.

4

THE BUSINESS PLAN

Your shop window

Showing your business plan to a venture capitalist could be described as the investment world's equivalent to a Broadway audition, but with the patience and understanding taken out. You get one, brutally short chance to make an impression, there is no guarantee that the reader's mood that day will lead to a balanced, considered judgement and it may be that the last thing he needs this month is three or four days' work on a proposition which will probably not come off anyway.

But, imperfect as the venture capital market is, quality will eventually pay. A professionally prepared business plan which presents a sound proposal will attract investors. This chapter will guide you through the various roles the business plan plays, what to put in it and how to write it.

Why write a business plan?

The obvious answer—because you can't raise finance without one—is also the most relevant in the context of this book. However selling to investors is only one of the many roles a business plan plays, and to write one solely for that purpose is to miss an opportunity to crystallise and consolidate your commercial thinking.

The business plan should be your blueprint for the growth of the company. To be effective, it needs to be the common property of the entire management team. It should summarise your collective thoughts on:

- what you are going to do;
- who is going to do it;
- why you will be doing it;
- how it is going to be done, and
- when.

One of the major benefits of compiling a detailed plan is its function as a catharsis, bringing hidden reservations, woolly thinking, uncertain assumptions and differing opinions within your team into the open. Until you agree on every aspect of the business—or at least accept a colleague's more expert judgement—it doesn't go into the plan. Making sure that the plan covers every major aspect of the business will therefore force you to align your thinking in the important areas.

The investor and the business plan

The business plan is the core of the investment process. The venture capitalist will use it:

- to form an early view of the quality of your proposal;

- to form, by inference, a view on the quality of your management team;

- as the starting point for his detailed appraisal of the proposal;

- as a tool to persuade his colleagues to accept the proposal;

- as the basis for negotiating investment terms with you;

- to identify risk areas;

and once he has made the investment:

- as a guide to the likely nature and rate of growth of the business;

- as a reference, to what you said you were going to do.

The more closely the plan reflects reality, the more appropriate will be the terms on which any investor provides finance, the more realistic his expectations and the more comfortable your life is likely to be after the investment is made.

Of course there is usually, in some aspect of the plan, a conflict between the need to be honest and analytical and its role as a tool for selling to investors. The answer to this is to be truthful—but carefully!

This chapter concentrates on the aspects of writing a business plan which are aimed at enhancing its attractiveness to potential investors. If you write a plan for all of the other reasons we identified above, then it may well be too long to use as a selling document, containing sections which are irrelevant or go into too much detail. On the other hand, as we shall see below, the plan you send to investors may contain some selling elements that you do not require in an internal plan. The answer is to write your own internal plan first, and then, if necessary, produce an amended or abridged version to show to potential investors.

Who should write the plan?

There are a number of differing views on this. The only consistent response from the debaters seems to be 'the management, not the advisers', but we still see a large number of proposals written by intermediaries and advisers.

There are four good reasons not to let your advisers write the plan. The first is that to a large extent this foils the venture capitalist's use of the plan as an indication of management quality—it wastes an early opportunity to impress him. Also, the adviser will not know your business well enough to write authoritatively; no matter how much you help, the writer's lack of detailed knowledge of the business invariably seems to show through. A further problem is that to ask an outsider to write the plan implies that you, the management team, lack the intellect to prepare it yourselves. Finally, and most importantly, it diminishes the plan's credibility as the collective responsibility and property of the management team.

So you should write it yourselves, using professional advisers to embellish or support it as appropriate.

Of course there is an exception to this rule. There is no correlation between literary ability and business acumen; it is difficult to imagine Henry Ford writing eloquent market analyses and some will argue that the business world is divided into those who make money and those who can write clever things about it. If producing readable English is not one of your strengths, ask somebody else to write the plan, provided that the improvement in presentation would outweigh the disadvantages listed above.

A more difficult question is whether different parts should be written by the different, appropriate members of the management team, or whether one member, either the most literate or senior, should be responsible for compiling the team's thoughts. I feel that, if possible, each member should prepare his own part of the plan. By refusing to entrust parts of the plan to his colleagues, a managing director casts doubt on both his ability to delegate and the quality of his management team. However one member of the team should edit the document, rewriting where necessary to maintain a consistent style.

The contents

As I write, I have six different guides to writing business plans, each of which contains different suggestions about areas to cover and the order in which to cover them. So far as raising finance is concerned, the order in which the contents are presented is rarely crucial, provided that the opening two pages excite the reader's interest and that everything else is accessible with the various sections clearly labelled.

As a starting point, try the following list of headings:

1. Executive Summary

2. Background and Management Experience

3. Product/Service

4. Market

5. Marketing and Sales

6. Management Structure and Operations

7. Management

8. Financial History and Projections (summaries)

Appendices:

I   Management CVs
II Detailed forecasts and assumptions
III Market surveys, if appropriate and available
IV Detailed product descriptions, brochures, reviews, etc.

1. Executive summary

The summary is your fifteen second audition. Assume it will be read over a cup of coffee by a venture capitalist who has got to the end of his morning's post and whose mind is on a raft of problems to be solved before lunch. The summary's objective is to get him to read the rest of the plan on the train home that evening.

Checklist

The summary needs to tell the reader:

- the type of investment (see Chapter One);

- how much is needed;

- why;

- what your company does.

It should lead the reader to infer:

- that the management team is competent;

- that the company has a sound commercial strategy;

- that there is scope for long-term growth and an attractive return.

The summary is your hard sell. It should be written after the rest of the document is finished, so that it reflects the care you have taken with the plan and brings out its best elements.

You will need to make bold statements in order to create an impact, but ensure that they can be supported by factual evidence. For example:

'ZedCo has achieved faster revenue growth than any of its competitors over the last three years' (which can be proved statistically), or:

'We believe we have the most advanced and efficient distribution system of any company in our industry' (which the investor can check by using an external consultant)

are acceptable, while:

'We have achieved our aim of establishing excellence in our management team',

'Yico is now accepted as the best company in the industry',

are vague and, as subjective conclusions formed by biased insiders, carry no value.

2. Background and management experience

Venture capitalists use the word 'story' a lot; they say 'ZedCo has a good story', or 'the Yico proposal looks good on the surface but I don't believe the story.' This has developed because investing in a company is no more than a stage in that company's progress. The series of events and influences which have led the company to seek equity financing, the uses to which the financing will be put and the company's performance to date (collectively, the story) give the potential investor strong clues about its likely performance in the future.

This section is the chance to tell your story. It should build on the features which attracted the reader's interest in the executive summary. Keep it brief—three pages at most—and, as far as possible, in note or bullet point format. Solid chunks of narrative run the risk of being skimmed rather than read in full, and important points may be missed. Remember that in this section you are picking out the highlights and attractive features of your proposal.

Checklist

You should cover, in summary form, the following areas:

1. Your business's history, including:

   a) its founders
   b) its financing to date
   c) its financial performance.

2. The market opportunities it was created to exploit, including:

   a) the industry
   b) the features of your industry which influence strategy.

3. The developments in the market and the way your strategy has changed, including:

   a) setbacks
   b) achievements.

4. The company's strategy for the future (which should be a natural evolution from the previous point), including:

   a) what is changing?
   b) how is the market likely to grow?
   c) where is the competition?
   d) how the strategy has evolved
   e) any major events or discontinuities which make past performance or activities irrelevant as a guide to the future.

5. The background and experience of each member of the management team, including:

   a) when they joined the team
   b) what particular skills and strengths they bring
   c) how relevant is their experience.

This is your opportunity to impress the investor with the calibre of the team. Refer back to Chapter Two for a breakdown of the elements he will be looking for, and bring as many of them as possible out in this section.

3. Product or service

If the reader is still with you, he will be sufficiently interested in the proposal to follow a more detailed explanation of what it is you do, make or market.

This section of the plan is therefore the place to provide a full description of your range of products or services.

Checklist

Describe:

- what they do;
- who uses them;
- how they work;
- why they are better;
- what unique features they have;
- competitors' products or services;
- pricing policies;
- current development status;
- product lifespan;
- development plans;
- research and development plans and facilities;
- patent and licence situation;
- status of any appropriate regulatory approvals;
- appropriate safety, health or quality standards legislation.

Don't shy away from explaining in some depth: this section can comfortably run to six or seven pages if necessary. If it contains more than the reader requires he will move on, knowing that he has detailed answers available here when he needs them. However if purely technical explanations require more than three pages or so, summarise them here and either put the detail in an Appendix or offer to make it available to interested investors subsequently.

If you have any particularly striking photographs, extracts from product reviews or other clear evidence of your product or service's superiority then put it in this section, although bulky brochures and long reviews should be placed in an Appendix.

There should be no need to reveal confidential product information at this stage—never do so until you have a signed confidentiality agreement from the reader.

4. The market

The primary function of this section is to act as a background to the business strategy you outlined in Section 2. The market is one of the aspects of the proposal which will receive intense and detailed scrutiny, so that a reasoned, well researched and competent display of your understanding here, which is consistent with the research the investor will undertake independently, will make a significant positive impression.

Checklist

This section should review:

- the size and breakdown (by geography, customer type, product division or any other relevant criterion) of your market;

- recent and anticipated trends, in terms of both size of the market and its 'shape';

- major influences on the market;

- your existing and anticipated market share;

- a frank review of your major competitors, summarising relative strengths and weaknesses;

- a summary of your own customer base.

Break them down in the same way you broke down the market as a whole, so that the reader can see how you fit into each segment of the market.

5. Marketing and sales

If the previous section was strategic, then this is its tactical counterpart. It addresses the detail of how you will convert the opportunity you identified and described in Sections 1, 2 and 4 into profitable revenue.

Checklist

- Target customers. Who do you expect your customers to be in three or five years' time? Where will the growth come from? Being able to identify specific targets (major single customers for industrial, large unit sale products, or identifiable target groups for small unit or consumer goods) adds credibility to your definitions of market size and structure in the previous section.

- Buying methods. How is the buying decision made? Summarise typical:

decision-making and budget allocation processes,
lead times and order slippage,
order sizes,
tender processes,
approved supplier rules and requirements.

- Selling methods:

  Size of salesforce;
  Type of salesforce (reps, outside agents, commission only etc.)
    and remuneration basis;
  Geographic and segmental coverage of salesforce;
  Historic and forecast effectiveness of salesforce.

- Sales position:

  Current order book;
  Anticipated orders.

- Advertising and promotion:

  Advertising requirements and policy;
  Promotional activities.

6. Management structure and operations

You won't have mentioned the management team since Section 2, so now is the time to bring the reader's attention back to the people aspect of the proposal. This part of the plan therefore plays two roles; its overt function is to describe how the company is run, while indirectly it should continue to develop the message, which was introduced in Section 1 and will be driven home in Section 7, that your team is the best available to run it.

It is important to demonstrate not only how the business runs now, but that you have a clear idea about how it will run in three or five years' time. Identify your likely requirements and be frank about any potential problems in meeting them.

Checklist

This section will make the reader feel that he understands how your business works. It should cover:

- The management structure:

  Provide an organisation chart;
  Write a sentence or two summarising each of the management team's areas of responsibility.

- The production or service delivery process:

  Describe the process;
  Identify bottleneck or critical elements;
  Note major decision points;
  Summarise raw material sources;
  Note any major make or buy decisions;
  Summarise your quality control processes.

- Personnel:

  Identify who is responsible at each stage;
  Discuss particular skill requirements;
  Note any significant points regarding training, recruitment, staff
  turnover or any particular competitive advantage that the
  company enjoys in relation to its staff.

- Information technology:

  To what extent are your processes automated?
  How well do your systems cope?
  What are the requirements for the expansion envisaged by the
  business plan?
  What Management Information Systems exist and what will be
  needed in the future?

- Premises:

  Describe your premises and the basis on which you occupy
  them; if relevant, include a plan showing how your processes
  flow; summarise the requirements for your planned future
  expansion.

7. Management

Given the importance of the management, it may appear strange to
place them this far down the batting order. However in Sections 1 and
2 you will have given the reader some signals about the exceptional
qualities of your team, while the thoroughness with which the interven-
ing parts of the plan have been prepared will have given him increasing
confidence about the team. The role of this section is to provide the
hard evidence which will support his developing favourable judgement.

Detailed CVs for each member of the team will be contained in an
Appendix. This section should simply highlight the relevant specific
experience of each of your managers.

Checklist

- For each member of the team, describe:

  role (which will link back to Section 6);
  age, relevant experience and expertise;
  any appropriate qualifications.

- Identify particular strengths and weaknesses in the management team.

- Identify any existing or anticipated gaps in the team's combined skills set, and explain how these will be rectified.

- Describe each of the non-executive directors, summarising their relevant experience and their role in the company.

- Outline the personal financial contribution made by each member of the team, and his existing equity share in the business.

- Summarise the team's personal objectives.

8. Financial summaries

The financial information you present in this section can be broken down into three sections:

1. Historic results

These are likely to be the first independently verified commentary on your progress to date that the reader will come across. You should take no more than two pages to show summaries of the Profit and Loss Account and Balance Sheet for the last three years, if you have been established that long. If your most recent annual accounts have not yet been audited, include the summary here anyway, with a note on the status of the audit.

Supplement the figures with a commentary, explaining major trends and influences on the figures, cross-referring to other sections in the plan where possible, and sources of finance to date.

2. Recent management accounts and current budget

Show the month-by-month summarised Profit and Loss Account and Cashflow Statement since the end of the last financial year, together with the monthly budgets for these items for the entire year. Highlight and explain any significant variances from budget, and comment on the likelihood of achieving the year-end targets.

3.   Financial projections

Before showing figures to the reader, summarise the major assumptions
you have made about:

>   rate and source of revenue growth;
>   major influences on costs and their relationship to revenues;
>   structure and timing of funding;
>   interest costs;
>   other major financial factors identified earlier in your plan.

There is no guarantee that the investor will read this page first, but at
least this way there is a chance that he will understand the basis on
which your projections are prepared.

You should then show forecast profit and loss accounts, cashflow
summaries and balance sheets for at least the next three years, up to a
maximum of five. Show profit and loss and cashflow monthly for the
first year, quarterly for the second and annually thereafter. You only
need to show annual balance sheets.

The projections should occupy no more than five pages (one each for
the first year's profit and loss and cashflow, a further one each for subsequent years and a page of balance sheets). Do not include endless pages
of spreadsheets in this section; the detail behind these summaries can be
included in an Appendix or provided later if necessary.

Provide a commentary on the projections, identifying the major areas
of uncertainty and highlighting significant elements. The commentary
should give the reader comfort that the projections have been carefully
and thoughtfully prepared.

As part of your financial forecasting process you should have prepared a series of sensitivity analyses, showing the effect of various sales
levels, raw material prices, etc. Include a summary of the effects on
profit and cashflow of the most likely variances.

A sample business plan

The remainder of this chapter is comprised of extracts from a sample
business plan, based on a real life case.

HUTCHOUSE
DEVELOPMENTS
LIMITED

BUSINESS PLAN

AND

FINANCING PROPOSAL

July 1990

Contents

1.   Executive Summary

2.   Background

3.   Management

4.   Activities

5.   Market Trends

6.   Review of Existing Sites *(not reproduced here)*

7.   Historic and Projected Financials

8.   Potential Acquisitions

9.   Proposed Investment Terms

Appendices

Management CVs *(not reproduced here)*

Audited Accounts to December 1989 *(not reproduced here)*

Sample Site Plan and House Types *(not reproduced here)*

1. EXECUTIVE SUMMARY

Hutchouse was established in 1987 following a Management Buyout from Nonnie Properties. The Company was initially funded with equity of £1.5m, £100,000 of which was provided by the management team with the balance from a syndicate led by Vixen Ventures plc, and debt facilities totalling £8m provided by Rummidge Credit Bank plc.

An additional £412,000 of equity was subsequently subscribed by the management and investors, in tandem with an increase in total banking facilities to £9.125m.

At 31 December 1989 the Company held £8.3m of development land and work in progress and had drawn £6.2m of its bank facilities. Hutchouse was profitable in its first full year of trading and has remained so, despite the deterioration in market conditions during 1989.

In order to capitalise on the acquisition opportunities arising from the present condition of the housing market, the company wishes to raise a further £5m in Mezzanine and Equity finance. Vixen Ventures plc is acting as lead investor and co-ordinator for this funding round.

The Executive Directors of the Company have between them 64 years of experience in residential property development. A particular feature of the team is its ability to identify, negotiate attractive acquisition prices and obtain favourable planning consents on smaller sites (typically 10 to 100 units). These developments offer significant profit margins, as they are too small to attract competition from major developers but too large for local speculators, and allow the Company to exploit specific local demand.

The Non Executive Chairman is a main board director of a number of major quoted companies and has extensive industrial and property development experience.

Summarised Profit and Loss Account (£000s)						
Year to 31 Dec:	1988	1989	1990	1991	1992	1993
Turnover	2,395	2,266	2,356	14,402	22,179	30,190
Gross Profit (after interest)	500	599	475	1,684	3,316	4,956
Overheads	225	277	458	722	949	1,091
Profit Before Tax	275	322	17	962	2,367	3,865

The substantial revenue growth anticipated for 1991 arises primarily from the release for sale of units on a wide range of development sites which are currently under construction.

2.   BACKGROUND

The Company was formed in May 1987 for the express purpose of purchasing the three development sites which formed the land bank of the Residential Development Division of Nonnie Properties plc which was managed by the executive directors. It was these acquisitions, together with the purchase of two additional residential development sites that formed the basis of the business plan on which the Company obtained both institutional equity and bank funding.

Equity finance was organised by Vixen Ventures plc as lead investor and amounted to £1.4 million being provided by a mixture of Ordinary and Redeemable Preference Shares. The management invested a further £100,000.

Bank funding totalling £9.125 million is provided by Rummidge Credit Bank plc under a Master Credits Agreement dated October 1987 and subsequently amended by letter dated February 1989 and provides specific development finance, overdraft and performance bond facilities.

The Share Subscription Agreement included a ratchet mechanism by which management share-holding could be increased by redemption of investors' Redeemable Ordinary Shares based on the achievement of specific targets. To date, certain of these targets have been achieved and in July 1990 a number of Redeemable Ordinaries were repurchased by the Company. The remainder of the arrangement has been terminated. Also in July 1990 a further £412,000 of equity was subscribed; £100,000 by the Chairman, £124,500 by the executive management and £187,500 by the Institutional Investors. Details of the current share structure are given elsewhere in this document.

The Company has continued to be active within the residential property market since 1987 and today owns 11 development sites, all with full detailed planning located throughout the Midlands. On six of the above sites work has started and is continuing at a level consistent with current demand. It is expected that work will commence on the remaining five sites during the course of 1990. The total number of housing plots held by the Company at 31 December 1989 was 282.

3. MANAGEMENT

The management of the Company is undertaken by the executive directors who are the Company's original promoters, all of whom have considerable experience in both construction and residential property development. Day to day direction and control is exercised via an executive committee. In addition to the executive directors, the Company employs the full time services of a Chartered Quantity Surveyor.

Strategic direction of the Company is influenced and monitored by two non-executive directors appointed by the external investors and a newly appointed independent non-executive chairman.

Non Executive Chairman
ANTHONY PLEDGE, MA, FCA (age 55)
Until the early 1980s, was Managing Director of International Consumer Plastics plc. Is non executive director of three major quoted companies and chairman of a quoted property developer.

Executive Directors
GRAHAM CHATTEL, FCCA (age 53)
Managing Director with overall responsbility for direction and control of the Company's operations. Also has specific responsibility for financial control and liaison with investors, bankers and the Company's professional advisers.

Previous experience includes a position as Managing Director of a major development subsidiary of Big Co. plc.

ALAN GROUT (age 47)
Executive Director, a member of the executive committee with special responsibility for product development and sales and marketing.

Was previously Managing Director of the residential property development division of Nonnie Properties plc.

JOHN JOIST (age 38)
Executive Director, a member of the executive committee with special responsibility for the day to day management of current developments.

Previous experience includes Executive Director of the residential development subsidiary of a major insurance company.

Non Executive Directors
A.D. VICE (age 62)
Property consultant. Formerly Deputy Chief Executive and Director of Administration, City of Rummidge and subsequently Managing Director, Rummidge Economic Development Corporation.

QUENTIN FIX (age 29)
Executive Director of Vixen Ventures plc.

4.   ACTIVITIES

Geographical Focus

The main thrust of the company's development to date has been largely in the Midlands area although the Company has also undertaken developments in both the Manchester and Cleveland areas.

The Company is prepared to undertake developments throughout the whole of England and Wales excluding the Greater London area. However the main element behind a decision to develop in any particular location is local knowledge.

The Company will not make a decision to invest in any development site unless it has been able to acquire a significant level of local knowledge. As the Company does not generally purchase land via tender or auctions, this local knowledge would normally have helped with the introduction to the prospective seller. The Company's sources of local knowledge are, wherever appropriate, linked with the eventual development. Therefore, local contacts are generally solicitors, estate or land agents, architects and builders, which are resident, well established and active in the local area.

This approach allows both the Company and the development to be more readily accepted and regarded as a local development. It benefits from the close links that the local contacts will have with the local authorities and their detailed knowledge of local conditions.

Type of Site - Market Positioning

The principal house units developed by the company fall into three categories:

1.   Homes for first time buyers.

2.   Middle range 3 & 4 bedroom homes suitable for second/third time buyers trading up.

3.   Bungalow type accommodation suitable for early retirement, but not being wardened or sheltered accommodation.

However, the majority of the units developed by the Company fall into the second named category, being the family type house of three to four bedrooms and having an average selling price in the region of £80,000.

The Company has a specific policy of avoiding high risk/high reward type developments.

The size of development undertaken by the Company is linked to the desire, wherever possible, to purchase by private treaty and to avoid paying open market prices for land. This is achieved by exploiting a niche in the market, concentrating on development sites of between say 10 - 100 units which, in the main, are too large for the local builder and too small to interest the major national house building companies.

Site Purchase, Planning Permission, Development & Sale

Site Purchase

As has been stated earlier, the majority of the Company's site purchases are undertaken by private treaty negotiations but by whatever means the site is acquired, the same procedure is adopted to determine the suitability of the site and to ensure that the development will meet the Company's financial criteria. These procedures can be summarised as follows:

* Site visit to determine general suitability.

* Market research to establish local need, competition and indicative selling prices.

* Discussions with local authority planners, road authorities and essential services to establish local government views and needs.

* Discussion with chosen architect as to type of site layout that can be achieved. These discussions will result in a sketch layout being prepared.

* Local research with local authority, NHBC and local builders to establish local ground conditions and current building prices.

* From the above research a Development Financial Appraisal is prepared to the Company's criteria on minimum profit per unit and minimum return on expect maximum capital employed.

  The Development Financial Appraisal is the basis for calculating an acceptable land cost. Once this has been determined it provides the background for establishing land purchase price, either with the current owner in purchases by private treaty or the figure to be used for tender for auction purposes.

* Following subject to contract agreement on price, or prior to submission in the case of tenders or auctions, the Company's solicitors will carry out all the normal enquiries associated with land purchases.

* During this period also the Company will undertake soil tests on the site and reassess the Development Financial Appraisal.

* The Development Financial Appraisal, together with a valuation in support of the land price, is then submitted to the Board and the Company's bankers for approval to purchase.

Planning Permission

The Company as a matter of policy does not generally purchase any land which is not at least zoned for residential development.

The Company will, however, purchase options on non-zoned land where, in the opinion of the management, it has a good chance of achieving planning permission within the option period.

As mentioned above, discussions with local authority planners are opened as soon as a serious decision has been taken to consider the purchase of the development site.

These discussions will continue after purchase of the development site based on the sketch layout and will lead to the Company applying for firstly outline planning permission and then full detailed planning permissions for the development site.

The Company has a 100% success rate in achieving full detailed planning permission (without the necessity for planning appeals) on its development sites for the number of housing units envisaged by its development appraisals.

The Company's interest in planning approval does not stop with the granting of full detailed planning on any particular development. Throughout the construction period of a development the Company will continue to assess with its local advisors local need and changing market conditions and, if and when appropriate, revised planning permission will be obtained.

Site Development

The Company's basic philosophy for site development is that each development should conform to good planning, design and building practice and be fully covered by both the builders' and the Company's NHBC registration.

In selecting a builder for any development the Company is seeking to obtain value for money from a builder of good local reputation, thereby enhancing the standing of the development.

Building contracts take the form of fixed price contracts for the phased construction of each development, thereby allowing the Company to remain in full control of the speed at which any particular site is developed.

Payment under the contracts are made against Quantity Surveyors' certificates for completed stages of work only. This ensures that the risks attached to the loss of unfixed materials on site remain firmly with the builder. The Company also hold monetary retention on the builder to cover remedial work during the building maintenance period.

Sale

It is the general policy of the Company to appoint local selling agents for each of the development sites at the commencement of the development and to consult with that agent through to the completion of the total development. The agent is, therefore, included in discussions as to number of units, size and type of units, general site layout and pricing of the units for sale.

The normal practice is not to offer the units for sale until such time as a completed or near completed unit is available for prospective purchasers to view. Where the number of units on a development indicate the need, a fully furnished show house will be made available. Currently, show houses have been established on the following four developments: Caxton Park & Greenlands Park, Sheringham, Mundersely and Metfield.

In the present sales climate the Company does not accept reservations until the prospective purchaser has a completed chain in respect of the sale of their own home.

The Company currently offers a mortgage subsidy package for early exchange of contract worth £2,100 over a two year period. However, it does not contemplate at this time the adoption of either Shared Equity or Part Exchange schemes.

5.   MARKET TRENDS

House types & standards

As stated elsewhere, the main house product of the Company has been and will remain the 3/4 bedroom home, normally detached or semi-detached with garage and garden.

It is a product that appeals to the second/third time mover as they seek to improve their housing standard. This is the largest sector of the new housing market.

The Company continuously monitors market trends to ensure that its product remains fresh, up to date and has the kerb appeal that will ensure continuing interest from the buying public.

We do not, however, consider it necessary to fill the house with add-on attractions such as fully fitted kitchens, except perhaps in flats or apartment developments. The basic concept is a good quality, well designed home at the lowest possible selling price. This is based on the philosophy that people trading up wish to obtain maximum benefit from such a move by way of additional space, additional bedrooms, ensuite bathroom, etc. and will often keep their existing white goods.

Market trends

Another advantage the Company has is linked to the local input that we seek in each of our developments. This means that while we, as a national based company, can continue to be aware of national trends in house design and purchasers needs, the local input from estate agents, architects and/or builders, ensures that even our standard houses are modified to reflect local needs and fashions.

Statistical trends

Despite the current market conditions, there remains a consistent, long term requirement for additional housing stock. This is due to demographic factors, changes in the pattern of family life and changes in social patterns reflected in the following tables.

From the statistics below it will be seen that live births continue to exceed registered deaths and that the population numbers in the age groups 15-19, 20-24 and 25-29 (i.e. potential new house buyers) considerably exceed the population numbers in the age groups 30-34, 35-39 and 40-44 (existing house owners).

It will also be seen from the NHBC first time buyer ability to buy index, reproduced below, the effect that:

    1)   the substantial increases in house prices during late 1988 and 1989 had
             on the index;

2) the equally fast effect that falling or static house prices linked to buyers average earnings increasing by 9-10% per year has had on the index during the third and fourth quarter 1989 and first quarter 1990.

We expect to see a further sharp upward movement in the index when the second quarter 1990 figures are published.

First Time Buyer Ability to Buy Index
(The higher the index, the greater the ability to buy)

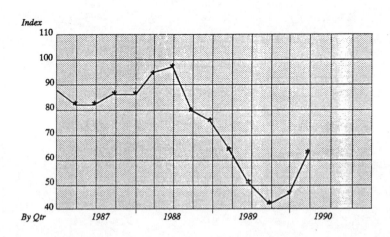

Source: NHBC

Age Distribution : 30 June 1988

Resident Population (000s)

Age	England & Wales	United Kingdom
0- 4	3287	3747
5- 9	3164	3619
10-14	2957	3394
15-19	**3717**	**4249**
20-24	**4155**	**4728**
25-29	**3966**	**4495**
30-34	3430	3892
35-39	3414	3847
40-44	3753	4006
45-49	2827	3209
50-54	2699	3055
55-59	2651	3000
60-64	2607	2940
65-69	2555	2865
70-74	1929	2166
75-79	1661	1860
80-84	1072	1196
85 over	659	796

Source: CSO

Live Births/Registered Deaths (United Kingdom) (000s)

	Births	Registered Deaths
1983	721	659
1984	730	645
1985	751	671
1986	755	661
1987	776	644
1988	788	649
1989	772	N/A

Source: CSO

7. HISTORIC AND PROJECTED FINANCIALS

Profit & Loss Account

£000s Year to 31 December:	Actual 1988	Actual 1989	Budget 1990	Forecast 1991	Forecast 1992	Forecast 1993
Sales						
No.	26	30	34	187	273	370
Value	2,395	2,266	2,536	14,402	22,179	30,190
Cost of Sales						
Development Costs	1,625	1,475	1,686	10,363	16,615	22,718
Interest	183	188	278	2,079	2,113	2,419
Joint Venture	87	4	97	276	135	97
TOTAL	1,895	1,667	2,061	12,718	18,863	25,234
Development Profit	500	599	475	1,404	2,886	4,366
Inflation Allowance	0	0	0	280	430	590
Net Development Profit	500	599	475	1,684	3,316	4,956
Overheads	(256)	(287)	(444)	(568)	(632)	(684)
Interest:						
Received	49	42	0	296	133	43
Overdraft	(2)	(16)	(2)	0	0	0
Mezzanine	0	0	0	(450)	(450)	(450)
Equity Loan	(16)	(16)	(12)	0	0	0
NET INTEREST	31	10	(14)	(154)	(317)	(407)
Net Profit Before Tax	275	322	17	962	2,367	3,865
Corporation Tax	40	76	6	337	828	1,353
	235	246	11	625	1,539	2,512
Preference Share Dividends	0	0	0	252	252	240
RETAINED PROFIT	235	246	11	373	1,287	2,272

Balance Sheet

£000s 31 December	Actual 1988	Actual 1989	Budget 1990	Forecast 1991	Forecast 1992	Forecast 1993
Fixed Assets	34	26	26	10	2	2
Current Assets						
Development Properties	5,466	8,300	12,936	17,305	17,787	26,018
LESS:						
Development Loans	(4,485)	(5,799)	(9,142)	(13,023)	(12,660)	(19,009)
	981	2,501	3,794	4,282	5,127	7,009
Debtors	446	207	629	2,300	4,164	3,816
Bank Deposits	949	148	0	0	0	0
Bank Account	(346)	(270)	580	1,849	149	439
	1,049	85	1,209	4,149	4,313	4,255
Current Liabilities						
Creditors	425	650	686	1,050	1,061	966
Corporation Tax	40	117	8	183	529	1,053
	465	767	694	1,233	1,590	2,019
Net Current Assets	1,565	1,819	4,309	7,198	7,850	9,245
Mezzanine Debt	0	0	0	2,500	2,500	2,500
NET ASSETS	1,599	1,845	4,335	4,708	5,352	6,747
	=====	=====	=====	=====	=====	=====
Capital & Reserves						
Ordinary Shares	182	182	529	529	529	529
Red Ordinary Shares	218	218	0	0	0	0
'A' Pref Shares	1,100	1,100	1,100	1,100	550	0
'B' Pref Shares	0	0	319	319	319	159
'C' Pref Shares	0	0	2,200	2,200	2,200	2,200
	1,500	1,500	4,148	4,148	3,598	2,888
Equity Loan	100	100	0	0	0	0
Profit & Loss Account						
B/Forward	(236)	(1)	245	187	560	1,754
Current Year after Tax	235	246	11	373	1,287	2,272
Share Premium Acc	0	0	131	0	(93)	(167)
Net Capital	0	0	(200)	0	0	0
Expenses						
	(1)	245	187	560	1,754	3,859
TOTAL CAPITAL & RESERVES	1,599	1,845	4,335	4,708	5,352	6,747
	=====	=====	=====	=====	=====	=====

Key Figures

£000s *Monthly Balances*	*Budget* *1990*	*Forecast* *1991*	*Forecast* *1992*	*Forecast* *1993*
Overdraft Cash Forecast				
January	(154)	2,715	1,815	(14)
February	(176)	2,695	1,804	226
March	(208)	2,401	1,572	396
April	(217)	2,038	1,173	420
May	(259)	1,762	878	458
June	(204)	1,162	547	313
July	(252)	1,360	143	96
August	(216)	1,720	203	282
September	(307)	1,786	(19)	223
October	1,251	1,885	(89)	201
November	896	1,963	28	467
December	580	1,849	149	439
Development Loan				
Forecast				
January	(5,929)	(10,034)	(12,869)	(12,920)
February	(6,011)	(10,091)	(13,557)	(13,236)
March	(6,110)	(10,785)	(14,083)	(14,097)
April	(6,037)	(11,445)	(14,403)	(14,952)
May	(6,152)	(11,908)	(14,784)	(15,711)
June	(6,024)	(12,009)	(14,266)	(16,506)
July	(6,769)	(11,392)	(14,381)	(17,425)
August	(6,733)	(10,971)	(13,897)	(18,266)
September	(6,995)	(11,220)	(13,367)	(17,766)
October	(7,489)	(11,701)	(13,337)	(18,477)
November	(8,430)	(12,398)	(12,710)	(18,626)
December	(9,142)	(13,023)	(12,660)	(19,009)
Land Bank: No. of Units				
B/Forward	282	408	581	588
Purchased in Year	160	360	280	720
Sold in Year	34	187	273	370
C/Forward	408	581	588	938
Interest included in				
Development Costs				
B/Forward	910	1,684	1,388	1,482
Added in Year	1,052	1,783	2,207	2,555
Deducted in Year	278	2,079	2,113	2,419
C/Forward	1,684	1,388	1,482	1,618

Management Accounts
Quarter to 31 March 1990

£000s *Summary Profit & Loss Account*	*Actual*	*Budget*
Sales		
No. of Units	8	3
Value	546,500	217,400
	======	======
Income		
Scheme Profits*	125,266	48,400
Less J/V Provision	24,390	8,600
Less Management Res.	0	0
SUB TOTAL	100,876	39,800
Bank Interest	3,623	0
Scheme Man. Fees	28044	28,000
GROSS PROFIT	132,543	67,800
	======	======
Costs		
Overheads	99,716	105,700
Overdraft Interest Payable	13,526	14,000
	113,242	119,700
	======	======
NET PROFIT BEFORE TAX	19,301	(51,900)
	======	======

*After charging financial costs

Management Accounts
Balance Sheet
31 March 1990

	£	£
Fixed Assets		
Fixture & Fittings	11,406	
Equipment	12,781	

		24,187
Current Assets		
Development Properties	8,308,918	
Land Options	6,460	
LESS: Loans	(6,089,706)	

	2,225,672	
	451,361	
Debtors	(287,097)	
Bank Current Account	171,361	
Bank Deposit Account	------------	
TOTAL CURRENT ASSETS		2,561,297
Current Liabilities	47,920	
Trade Creditors	6,755	
Corp. Tax Curr. Year	661,431	
Sundry Creditors	------------	
		716,106

NET ASSETS		1,869,378
		=======
Capital		
Ord. Shares		181,818
Red. Pre Ord. Shares		218,182
Pref. Shares		1,100,000

		1,500,000
Standard Equity Loan		100,000
Deferred Taxation		12,043
Profit & Loss Account		
Carried Forward 1/1/90	244,789	
Current Year		
Corp.Tax Curr.Year @ 35%		
		257,335

		1,869,378
		=======

8. POTENTIAL ACQUISITIONS

The Company will use the additional equity and mezzanine funding, linked with conventional bank development finance to continue to acquire and develop residential development sites within the 10-100 unit number bracket.

Again, it must be stressed that the Company is and will remain a residential property developer as opposed to builder. It will retain the flexibility to undertake developments in a number of regions of the country without the necessity of incurring the substantial fixed cost base associated with the running of a building operation.

The Company's approach to acquisitions will remain unchanged from that currently employed, the main points of which are summarised under the *Site Purchase* sub-heading within the *ACTIVITIES* section of this report.

For the purposes of the financial projections within the report, we have adopted a plan standard site. This represents a site capable of obtaining planning permission for 40 housing units, either houses or bungalows, selling in the market for an average price of £80,000 per unit. A copy of the standard appraisal for such a site is attached and shows that the Company would expect to make approx. £10,000 per unit which would provide a return on total costs of 14.3% and a return on maximum cash requirement of 24.5%. The financial projections generally assume that such a site would take approximately 34 months from date of purchase to date of sale of the last unit. However, we have also taken the view that in the current housing climate it will be possible to purchase some sites where planning permission acceptable to this Company has already been obtained and in these sites it has been assumed that the length of development period can be reduced to 29 months. The business plan has therefore been based on an average of 33 months from site purchased to final completion.

The Company is currently investigating a number of potential site and or company acquisitions and believe that it can achieve the housing unit plot purchases summarised below on which the financial projections are based.

	Total No. of Standard Plan Site Purchase	Total No. of Standard Plan Units Purchased
1990	4	160
1991	9	360
1992	7	280
1993	18	720

Plan Standard Site

Sales Details

Type	No.	Sq.Ft.	Total Sq.Ft.	Selling Price	Total Selling	Ave. Unit	Ave. Unit 70% Funding
Houses }	40	910	36,400	80,000	3,200,000		
Bungalows }	---		------------		------------	------------	------------
	40		36,400		3,200,000	80,000	80,000
	---		------------		------------	------------	------------

Cost Details

Land Cost					900,000	22,500	22,500
Building (Sq.Ft.)			36,400	} 37	1,338,271		
Road Costs (L.Mt.)				} 325	0		
				} 175	0		
Footpath/Ext. Costs				}	0		
Drainage				} 0	0		
White Goods (per unit)				} 0	0		
Landscaping				} 500	0	33,457	33,457
Legal & Prof (% of selling)			6.5	0	205,500	5,138	5,138

Finance

Build 6 mnths at 50% of ave cost @				16	68,263		
Pre Sale 2 mnths at ave cost @				16	41,967		
Land 3 years at 50% cost @			3	16	216,000	8,156	5,656
Contingency (per unit)			40	750	30,000	750	750
					------------	------------	------------
					2,800,000	70,000	67,500

Net Profit					400,000	10,000	12,500
					------------	------------	------------
					3,200,000	80,000	80,000
					------------	------------	------------

MAXIMUM CASH REQUIREMENT	1,576,000	
LAND AS % OF SELLING	28.13	28.13
NET PROFIT AS % OF SELLING	12.50	15.62
NET PROFIT AS % OF TOTAL COSTS	14.29	18.52
NET PROFIT AS % OF MAX CASH REQUIREMENT	25.38	

Cost and sales prices are stated at 1990 values on the assumption that both will move in line with RPI Index.

Plan Standard Site

Diary & Cash Flow (£000s)

Units	No.			
		Total Revenue	3,200	
		Total Land	900	
Houses & Bungalows	40	Total Other Costs	1,574	
		Total Interest	326	
		TOTAL PROFIT	400	

Diary						Cost		Revenue		Mnthly Total	Cum Total	Int @ 16 %	Rev Cum Total
Land Purch	Plann ing	Build	Build	Sell	Sell	Land	Other	Sales	Sales				
1 *						900	20			920	920	12	932
2										0	920	12	945
3										0	920	12	957
4										0	920	12	969
5										0	920	12	981
6										0	920	12	994
7	*						20			20	940	13	1026
8										0	940	13	1039
9		*					10			10	950	13	1061
10		*					68			68	1018	14	1143
11		*					68			68	1086	14	1225
12		*					68			68	1154	15	1309
13		*					60			68	1222	16	1393
14		*		*			68			68	1290	17	1478
15		*		*			68			68	1358	18	1564
16		*		*			68	80		-12	1346	18	1570
17		*		*			68	80		-12	1334	18	1576
18		*		*			68	160		-92	1242	17	1501
19		*		*			68	240		-172	1070	14	1343
20		*		*			68	240		-172	898	12	1183
21		*		*			68	240		-172	726	10	1021
22		*		*			68	240		-172	554	7	856
23		*		*			68	160		-92	462	6	770
24		*		*			68	240		-172	290	4	602
25		*		*			68	240		-172	118	2	432
26		*		*			68	160		-92	26	0	340
27		*		*			68	240		-172	-146	-2	166
28		*		*			68	240		-172	-318	-4	-10
29		*		*			68	160		-92	-410	-5	-108
30		*		*			68	160		-92	-502	-7	-206
31		*		*			68	160		-92	-594	-8	-306
32		*					28	80		-52	-646	-9	-367
33								80		-80	-726	-10	-457
34												57	-400
35													
36													
						-----	-------	-------	-------				-----
TOTAL						900	1574	3200	0				326
						===	====	====	====				===

Hutchcuse Developments Limited - Accounting Policies

A summary of the principal accounting policies of the Company is set out below.

Accounting Convention

The accounts are prepared under the historical cost convention.

Depreciation

Depreciation is provided on all tangible fixed assets at rates calculated to write off the cost of each asset in a straight line over its expected useful life, as follows:

Fixtures and fittings	-	20% per annum
Office equipment	-	20% per annum

Turnover

Disposals of property are considered to have taken place where, by the end of the accounting period, there is a legally binding, unconditional and irrevocable contract where, in the opinion of the directors legal completion will take place subsequent to the balance sheet date.

Stocks and work in progress

Stocks and work in progress are stated at the lower of cost and net realisable value. Cost includes the cost of land, direct materials, labour and attributable interest and overheads. Net realisable value is the price at which stocks can be sold in the normal course of business after allowing for the cost of realisation, and where appropriate, the cost of conversion from their existing state to a finished condition.

Taxation

The charge for taxation is based on the profit for the period, adjusted for disallowable items. Tax deferred or accelerated is accounted for in respect of all material timing differences to the extent that it is probable that a liability will crystallise.

Operating leases

Costs in respect of operating leases are charged in arriving at operating profit.

9. PROPOSED INVESTMENT TERMS

Equity Investors

A total of £2,500,000 of new equity to be subscribed as follows:

Issue of 200,000 £1 Ordinary Shares, representing 32.9% of the total authorised equity capital, at £1.50 per share (the price at which management and investors subscribed in the last round).

Issue of 2,200,000 £1 'C' Cumulative Redeemable Preference Shares at par. The 'C' Preference Shares will carry the following rights:

Redemption
In priority to Ordinary, 'A' and 'B' Preference Shares in the event of a sale or liquidation.
Otherwise, at par in six equal semi annual instalments, the first on 1 January 1994.

Dividend
An annual dividend of 10% pa on par value, net of associated tax credits, accruing from 1 January 1991, payable semi annually in arrears.

The proposed investment structure capitalises the Company as follows:

Ordinary Share capitalisation:	£ 911,854
"Money Back" capitalisation:	£4,521,854

Assuming a sale in March 1993, on a PE of 9 times fully taxed 1992 profits, an investment in this round would produce a compound IRR of 49% pa.

Mezzanine Lending Terms

To be negotiated. The returns to shareholders quoted above envisages the grant of 40,000 Ordinary Share options to the mezzanine lender, which combined with a fixed interest rate of 18% pa would yield an IRR of 30% to a mezzanine lender on the exit assumption outlined above.

5

MEETING PEOPLE

Choosing and approaching investors

The venture capital industry is awash with clichés which compare the relationship between a company and its investor to marriage. The analogy is often taken too far, but it is certainly true that if marrying for money is the most difficult way there is to make a living, then taking finance from the wrong investor can be the most miserable.

In case you think that all venture investors are pretty much the same, consider these comments:

'Our three investors are all different . . . one is very laid back, one seems to be a worrier, and one is . . . very energetic. [When choosing investors] look for people with their feet on the ground . . . identify problem solvers and avoid bureaucracy.'

John Watts

'They were all very different. Some gave us a grilling that became exhaustive and in the end were asking such ridiculous questions. [Others] . . . seemed to make judgements not on thousands of bits of paper but on people, assessment of human nature.'

Paul Smith

The British Venture Capital Association has a membership of 124 venture capital companies. The Association's Directory (at Appendix II), lists them all. Each is different, in terms of investment criteria, ownership, style and objectives and no more than a few are likely to qualify as your potential backers. Your proposal might be so specialised, long term or high risk that almost the entire venture capital community will have to decline it, or such a straightforward development capital opportunity that you will have dozens of investors fighting for it. Either way, the more appropriate the investor you choose, the better your chances of raising finance on the best terms and enjoying a satisfactory long-term relationship.

This chapter looks at the process of targeting, approaching and selling to the investor. There are two elements to the choice of an equity financier. The first is to identify the venture capital companies whose investment criteria most closely match your proposal, and so attract a range of offers of financing. The second is to choose the right partner from your clutch of suitors.

Types of venture capital company

Venture capital companies can be broken down into five main types.

1.   Independent

An independent venture capital company is one that is not connected by ownership to the providers of the funds it manages. An independent will typically be owned by its directors and staff, often with a shareholding held by an external investor which provided its start-up financing. There are also a few publicly quoted independents.

Independents raise money from pension funds, insurance companies and other major institutions, typically assembling subscriptions from a number of institutions into a pool of money called a Fund. A Fund will usually be raised with a specific investment focus. See below for a review of the various ways in which funds can specialise.

During 1989, 642 investments were made by independent venture managers, representing 35 per cent of the total unquoted investment activity for the year.

2.   Captive

A Captive (or Tied) venture capital house is one which is a subsidiary of a major financial institution, which provides all, or a significant proportion, of the funds it manages. A management which raises a portion of its funds independently of its institutional or bank parent is referred to as a Semi-Captive.

All of the four major clearing banks, plus many other commercial and merchant banks, have their own venture or development capital subsidiaries. Insurance and pension funds also commonly have unquoted equity management teams.

During 1989, captive investors made 391 investments, 21 per cent of the total.

3.   3i plc

3i (the name comes from 'Investors in Industry') has a category all to itself, primarily because of its size. It is jointly owned by the major clearing banks and raises finance primarily from issuing publicly quoted debt instruments. It is the largest investor in the United Kingdom, with a portfolio of 5,000 investments, a network of regional offices and 500 executives.

During 1989, 3i made 707 investments, or 38 per cent of the total.

4. Government agencies

The role of the government in providing equity for small companies has steadily diminished over the last decade. The final vestiges of state involvement are to be found in the Welsh and Scottish Development Agencies, which are both active and professional investors in their regions, and a number of local agencies, such as Greater London Enterprise.

During 1989, 78 investments, or 4 per cent of the total, were made by government agencies or government funded investors.

5. Business Expansion Scheme (BES)

The BES, which gives tax breaks to private investors in small businesses, was launched as the Business Start Up scheme in 1983, with its title subsequently changed to reflect the admissibility of established businesses. The scheme has not been a success in terms of providing a new source of funds for small businesses, with most private investors using it as a tax shelter device rather than a medium for making high-risk, high-return investments.

The restrictions on the terms on which investments can be made, the minimum length of time they must be held and the upper limit of £750,000 for most companies puts BES finance outside the range of most venture fund managers, although a number do manage BES funds.

During 1989, 37 investments, or 2 per cent of the total, were made under the BES rules. This excludes financings for Assured Tenancy schemes, which are primarily a tax shelter and outside the scope of this book.

Investment focus

Investors can specialise by:

1. Stage

Early stage investors concentrate on start-ups and young companies which have not yet achieved consistent profitability. As we identified in Chapter Two, these investments present a high risk/return profile. They generally require a significant degree of day-to-day support and involvement from the investor, as the management team is likely to be incomplete while every decision may be critical to the company's success. In addition, investors in early stage companies have to base their assessment on an analysis of the management strengths and market potential of the investee, without the benefit of an established trading record.

For all of these reasons, these investors' executive teams will tend to have a background of industrial and general management experience, and expect to contribute significantly to specific areas of the investee's operations.

Development capital investors will be seeking more mature investments, expecting a steady return across the portfolio rather than the mixture of spectacular gains and outright losses that characterise an early stage fund. This is the sector of the unquoted investment market that investors have so far found to be the most rewarding.

It has attracted a large number of funds, leading to competition to invest in genuinely established, profitable companies which can become quite fierce for a strong, well presented proposal. Investee companies' management teams, strategies and prospects are generally a little less challenging to analyse than those of companies with very little trading history. For these reasons, executives of venture capital companies in this sector tend to develop a slightly greater emphasis on skills in financial engineering and salesmanship, aiming to present investment terms and a post-investment relationship that the company seeking funds will find attractive.

Specialist buyout funds are a recent phenomenon, emerging during 1988 and 1989. Of the £1.7 bn raised by the unquoted investment industry during 1989, more than half was raised by funds seeking to make investments in MBOs larger than £20 million. The essence of many of these transactions is speed of movement (to compete with trade buyers for target companies) and the use of high levels of leverage. Consistent cash flow and profitability are essential elements of companies financed in this way, as we shall see in Chapter Six, and creative financial structuring skills, combined with realistic assessments of future cashflows, lie at the core of the investors' ability to make returns.

2.   Industry sector

Investors specialising in financing younger companies are more likely to develop industry specialisations, as the quality of the support they can provide to management teams is dependent upon the specific experience of their executives.

However, even later stage investors are likely to develop an expertise in or a taste for a specific range of industrial sectors, which might make your proposal of particular interest.

3.   Region

During 1987, 57 per cent of funds invested by the venture capital industry went to companies in London and the South East. This fell to 48 per cent in 1989, which at least marks a satisfactory trend for companies based outside this area. Venture investors based outside this area paid increasing levels of attention to the provinces, with Manchester, Birmingham and Leeds in particular playing host to a range of regionally centred funds.

The geographic expansion of the industry is taking place as a series of discrete steps, which is tending to distort local competitive markets temporarily, leading to the prospect of attractive funding terms for companies fortunate enough to be in the right place at the right time.

What to look for in an investor

So what should you look for when choosing and interviewing potential investors? Clearly the terms an investor proposes will be an overriding factor, and Chapter Six is devoted to this aspect of the transaction. However the quality of your partner or partners is going to be a significant influence on the future of your business, and there is a range of other factors you should take into account.

Although some of the considerations in the list below will not apply until you are deeply involved in negotiations, and others only well after the investment has been made, it is worth while to review them all now.

- People
- Investing experience
- Aftercare policy and capacity
- Follow-on capacity.

The quality of the *people* with whom they dealt was cited by all the entrepreneurs spoken to for this book as the single most important factor, after the terms of the investment, in choosing an investor and maintaining the quality of the relationship.

You will naturally develop preferences for dealing with some individuals rather than others, but it is also worth thinking about:

- Longevity—is your preferred investor representative about to move on?

- Authority—can you agree a deal in principle with him, needing only the formal approval of an investment committee, or is he only a channel for communicating with decision-makers at his office?

- Understanding—does he have, or is he developing, a sufficient understanding of your industry for him to react constructively when events do not go according to plan?

The venture capital company's *investing experience* will have a bearing on their view of you. Find out what experience they have had in your sector. Again, the deeper their understanding, the better the chances of a positive reaction to unforeseen events (and the more difficult for you to pull the wool over their eyes). Ask the venture capitalist to take you through his company's investment portfolio (within reason—the entire 3i portfolio would be rather daunting!). This will give you an indication of how the company has developed its investment policy over the years and enable you to explore the types of deals with which it is most comfortable and competent.

The investor's *aftercare policy and capacity* also needs to be understood. Can he offer constructive support, such as introductions, help with arranging bank facilities, strategic input and assistance with senior personnel issues?

Does the investor want a seat on the board, and why? Find out how much information he expects after making the investment.

You should speak to some of the investor's existing investee companies, whose viewpoint may well differ from the investor's sales pitch.

Finally, consider the investor's *follow on capacity*; how deep is his pocket and will he be able to dig into it if you require further funding? What will the investor's attitude to further funding be in a variety of circumstances? Coming back for more cash to finance a growing, successful business is not a difficult proposition, but how will the venture capitalist react if you need further funding to cover a year's slippage in sales growth, or a production problem? You are unlikely to get a very helpful answer from the executive; again it will be useful to speak to some of his existing investee companies who have been through the process.

Remember that a venture capital backed company, whose existing investors will not or cannot provide the further funding it needs, is in an extremely weak position to raise further equity elsewhere; even if it succeeds in doing so, the terms will be punitive.

WHAT MORE COULD YOU POSSIBLY PUT INTO BUILDING YOUR BUSINESS?

You already have a successful business, but are now seeking support to help you go further—maybe finance for a new factory and new equipment, or perhaps market and product development.

British Steel (Industry) has already helped over 3,000 businesses to start up or expand in traditional steel areas, and we have further finance available for viable projects.

So if you have a thriving business, and some bigger ideas, call us today on 081-686 2311. It could be the most profitable business contact you've ever made.

BRITISH STEEL (INDUSTRY) LTD,
CANTERBURY HOUSE, 2-6 SYDENHAM ROAD, CROYDON CR9 2LJ. TEL: 081-686 2311.

British Steel industry

HELPING TO BUILD BUSINESSES.

Syndication

A president of one of the major US banks was once quoted as saying that 'no deal is so good that we want all of it'. This most certainly does not apply to the unquoted investment community, where the trend over the last two years or so, at least for development capital proposals, has been 'if it's half decent, we'll keep it all.'

Nevertheless, there are some good reasons why venture capitalists will syndicate an investment, inviting one or more other houses to take a portion. These include:

Amount It is unusual for funds to invest in excess of £3–4 million, although there are some notable exceptions (the Directory indicates the range of transaction sizes each investor is willing to consider). The upper limit for an investment from a particular fund is governed by that fund's size and the extent to which it wishes to diversify its portfolio. Most funds have rules which prevent them investing more than a certain percentage of the fund's total value (usually somewhere between 5 and 10 per cent) in any single company.

Funds which specialise in high-risk investments generally seek as wide a range of investments as possible, and a maximum investment of £500,000 in a start-up or early stage investment is not uncommon.

Combined Experience If a venture capital house receives a proposal which, though attractive, is in an industry sector of which it has no knowledge, it may well choose to invest in conjunction with another investor whose executives have more relevant experience.

Avoidance of control The mathematics of investing are such that sometimes the investor would require more than 50 per cent of a company in order to project a sufficient return. Although the management may well be content with a joint stake of less than this, they are as likely to be uncomfortable running a subsidiary of a financial institution as the institution would be in having a controlling interest.

Again, the answer is to spread the investment across more than one institution.

There are some advantages to the entrepreneur or management team in receiving financing from a syndicate of investors:

Broader range of support To have two, three or four financial institutions concerned with your welfare has to be better than having one. It multiplies the range of contacts, ideas and support available.

Lessened dependence on a single decision-maker Every company and individual is prone to outbreaks of unreasonableness. You are less exposed to the dangers of a personality clash with, or perverse decision-making by, a financier if you have more than one to appeal to.

Deeper pockets Further rounds of funding will be easier to arrange if the burden is spread across more than one investor.

Varying types of support Different venture capitalists have different strengths. You may find the aggressive, rapid deal-making skills of one investor balanced by the steadier counsel and broader experience of another.

In an investing syndicate, it is usual for there to be a Lead Investor. The lead is responsible for proposing and negotiating investment terms, leading the appraisal and due diligence process and negotiating the legal documents. You will therefore deal with a single venture capital company for most of the time, which will unofficially represent the entire syndicate.

If a clear leader of the syndicate does not emerge, insist that one is appointed. It is up to the investors to ensure that you do not have to repeat yourself in separate meetings (other than the initial sessions, when each venture house will be forming its own, preliminary view of your proposal) and that you can negotiate with a representative of the whole group.

Choosing and using intermediaries

If you have extensive and up-to-date knowledge of the unquoted equity markets, considerable financial negotiating experience, an intimate understanding of the fine points of investment structuring and are able to neglect your business for three to six months, you do not need to appoint an intermediary (nor do you need this book).

(In this chapter, we use the term 'adviser' as a synonym for a fund-raising intermediary. Professional advisers—the accountants and lawyers who will act for you with respect to the technical aspects of closing the financing—perform a different role, although one firm may act in both capacities. Chapters Seven and Eight review the roles of these professional advisers.)

What does an adviser do?

Help write the business plan

A intelligent but relatively uninformed outsider, the adviser is in a position to appraise the plan, objectively, from a potential investor's point of view, identifying weaknesses and inconsistencies.

Despite the rule about the plan being written by the team the adviser will often be able to add a little gloss and certainly to phrase the executive summary in such a way that the investor reads the rest of the plan.

Provide an independent strategic viewpoint

It is not uncommon for an experienced, commercially sound adviser to act as a sort of unofficial non-executive director during the phase of positioning the company for fund raising. As with the business plan, an outsider's view can throw a new light on issues that the executive team have drawn into a logjam.

Advise on potential investors

The adviser knows the market—the good ones spend a great deal of time talking to investors and watching the venture capital industry.

In addition to identifying the venture capital companies likely to find your proposal attractive, the adviser should be able to guide you on their various funds, objectives and styles.

Make introductions

Having the support of a high quality adviser adds to your credibility. It does not guarantee that you will raise money, but it generally does guarantee you the opportunity to talk to investors. Venture capitalists will always be careful to pay attention to intermediaries, who after all are often their major sources of business. The knowledge that an important provider of introductions will scrutinise his reaction to a proposal is likely to make an investor read your business plan that little more carefully.

Advise on and negotiate terms

An adviser will be able to give you an indication of the terms on which you are likely to be able to raise finance. He may often design a proposed investment structure to be incorporated in your business plan, although investors will often insist on proposing their own (if only to demonstrate who is really calling the shots).

He will usually take the lead in financial negotiations, using his knowledge of the market and understanding of the implications of the competing offers to improve the terms available. An important part of this process is explaining to you the deeper implications of different structures, so that you can decide which to accept based on a total understanding of what is on offer.

Lessen the management burden

By acting as a conduit for the routine requests for information which will flow from your potential investors, the investor can significantly reduce the time you spend on fund raising. He will often be able to interpret requests for information, so that you can follow the venture capitalist's thinking and decision process.

Manage the investment process

The adviser will keep the process moving, and should attempt to manipulate events so that you receive a number of outline offers within a few days of each other. He will guide you on how many venture capitalists to approach, when to cut down the number with whom you negotiate and when to make the decision to commit to one.

Choosing an adviser

If this sounds like an advertisement for advisers, it is more a tribute to the best intermediaries, who provide a valuable service to both investors and companies seeking finance. But finding the best one can be the difficult part.

The two main criteria are personal chemistry and a successful track record in raising finance for similar proposals.

Interview a number of potential intermediaries and speak to past clients of the one or two you feel most comfortable with. Explore the finance raising record not only of the firms you prefer, but the specific individuals who will be working with you.

Advisers' fees

The bulk of an intermediary's fee should be contingent upon a successful fund raising, although most of the successful advisers will expect a retainer.

Make sure that you understand exactly the basis on which the final, contingent fee will be calculated. This will normally be some combination of the amount of the financing and the time spent working on the proposal.

If there is a time-based element, agree with the adviser the extent of his involvement and the time he expects to charge you for. Even the most reputable firms will sometimes come and sit in at meetings when you don't really need them, confident that once the investment has closed they can add the time to their fee. You will probably feel, for example, that having your intermediary present while the potential investor explores your business plan, personal histories and strategy is unnecessary, while you will almost certainly want him there when discussing investment terms.

It is worth while to ask for a regular update of the likely total fee in the event of a successful closing; I have seen more than one successful completion meeting soured by the presentation of a fee from the fund raising adviser which, although in line with the terms agreed some months before, was very substantially larger than the company had expected.

6

TALKING TERMS

A guide to investment structuring

There is a continuing debate in the unquoted equity industry about the importance of investment structuring—the use by investors of a variety of share types, each carrying different and specific rights. The view at one pole is that fancy share structures are irrelevant; if the company does well, all concerned make money, if not then the investors will lose all their investment because, as equity holders, they are at the bottom of the heap for repayment.

The opposite view is that clever financial engineering can cater for all possibilities other than outright failure of an investee company, providing the investor with a number of ways of getting his money back with a return. This enables him to make investments which would otherwise appear to carry too high a risk or offer an inadequate reward.

The case of Plunder Ltd in Chapter One demonstrated how all parties can benefit from a constructive approach to structuring the equity investment. You will recall that the structure finally adopted had the effect of narrowing the likely range of the investor's anticipated return; it protected his investment in the event of the company underperforming but reduced his potential return if it sold for a higher price than that anticipated.

Of course, juggling the company's internal financing structure did not alter the overall level of risks and rewards the investment offered, but simply reallocated them between the investors and management. The management team lost the 'instant' paper profit they made by virtue of the investor valuing the company more highly than the terms of their own share subscription, and they now run the risk of losing a portion of their own investment if the company is sold for the same price as that at which it was bought.

In exchange for this, the team is rewarded with a larger percentage of the equity, offering the prospect of greater financial gain if the company succeeds.

This is the heart of financial structuring—allocating degrees and types of risk, together with their attendant potential rewards, to those parties best equipped to deal with them.

This chapter looks in a little more depth at the tools which can be used to structure an equity investment. An essential and integral part of the overall financing package, however, is the debt element, and we shall first review some considerations relating to loans.

How much should we borrow?

Until some time in 1988, the answer to the question of how much debt, as opposed to equity, finance to raise generally seemed to be 'as much as possible'. Debt is, as was discussed in Chapter Three, cheaper than equity from the shareholders' point of view. The more that can be borrowed, the less equity finance is required and therefore the greater proportion of a company's equity the management can expect to retain.

The catch, of course, is the extent to which high levels of borrowing place a fixed cashflow and cost burden on the company, and exacerbate the effects of any fluctuations in your trading performance. See Example 1a (p. 122) for the next stage in the Plunder buyout, which demonstrates the effects of two different levels of debt finance.

The consequence of the higher level of borrowings in Example 1b (p. 124) is an increased sensitivity in the shareholders' returns to changes in trading profits. A relatively small decrease in sales threatens to wipe out the company's profits at the pre-tax level. However, the management team benefits to a greater extent from any improvement in trading profits, over and above the forecasts, because it now holds a larger proportion of the equity.

This use of financial instruments to exaggerate the effect of underlying performance is called leverage. The Americans also use the word leverage to describe the level of debt a company carries; the equivalent UK term is gearing. Gearing can be measured, broadly, in three ways—by referring to the balance sheet, the interest burden on the profit and loss account and the demands on the borrower's cashflow.

Balance sheet gearing refers to a company's total debt as a percentage of its total assets. This is primarily of interest to a lender, as it gives a crude indication of the level of assets available from which to repay his loans should the company fail (assuming, of course, that the balance sheet valuations of assets bear some relation to reality). As it is a static measure, only relevant should the company stop trading, it is of limited interest to the company's management or shareholders. Of more importance are the dynamic measures, which refer to interest and cashflow.

Interest cover

This is the ratio of Profit Before Interest (but after all other trading and fixed expenses) to the total interest charge. (You can see that for 1991 it is forecast to be 1.89:1 in Example 1a, and 1.48:1 in Example 1b.) Clearly the higher the ratio, the better the company's ability to withstand a patch of difficult trading. However the ratio needs to be looked at with an understanding of how your company's Profit and Loss Account behaves at different levels of turnover. For example, a company with high gross margins but a high level of fixed costs, which do not vary greatly with the level of revenues, is more exposed than one that has a large proportion of its expenses linked directly to sales. The high fixed cost company is in effect already leveraged, as each pound gained or lost in revenue makes a substantial difference to the Profit Before Interest, and therefore needs to budget a greater margin of comfort at the interest cover level.

Debt service cover

This is the cashflow measure; it is the ratio of cash generated after all trading commitments (operating cashflow) to debt service obligations (interest and loan repayments). This is an even more significant indicator than the interest cover ratio of the company's ability to withstand a downturn. In difficult trading conditions cash, rather than profit, is the key to short-term survival. A company may default on interest cover covenants with the lender and start receiving its concerned attention, but when interest or principal payments are missed it runs a significantly greater risk of the bank taking drastic action to protect its security.

What is a safe level of debt?

Crudely, a level which can be serviced in a recession. Bearing in mind that over-optimism could lead to the failure of the company, compile a set of worst case forecasts which incorporate as many negative events as you can envisage happening together. Remember that bad news travels in packs—it is not coincidence that saw heavily leveraged retailers suffering from high interest rates at the same time as sales revenues reduced.

You should aim to borrow at a level which could be serviced by the trading profit and cashflow figures contained in these worst case budgets. This may result in your taking on board a lower level of debt than a bank is prepared to provide, raising more equity than seems necessary and thus reducing your share of the action. However, as any entrepreneur who has lived through an extended period with interest rates nudging 20 per cent and sales falling by the week will appreciate, a larger share of a failed company is worthless. The peace of mind that comes from knowing that the bank will not be considering the appointment of a receiver the minute sales fall off by 10 per cent also has to be worth the sacrifice of a little equity.

Mezzanine debt

As its name implies, mezzanine is a layer of debt that, in terms of the risk taken and rewards earned by the lenders, lies between conventional, secured borrowings and equity. (The term Mezzanine Financing has also been used to describe a round of equity finance for a company which is within a year or so of gaining a flotation. This use of the term is uncommon these days, probably because venture capitalists are becoming more cynical about companies which are 'almost ready to float'.)

The conventional, secured lender will have first call on the assets of the borrower as security, and is for this reason referred to as a senior lender (and his loan as senior debt). The mezzanine lender may have second charges over some of the company's assets, or be unsecured. Furthermore, repayments of mezzanine debt will not generally begin until a substantial portion of the senior debt has been repaid. His reward is generally a higher interest rate plus some options to purchase cheap Ordinary shares in the borrower, which enable him to make a profit when the investors achieve their exit. Example 2 (p. 126) demonstrates the use by Plunder of mezzanine debt.

The essential point to bear in mind is that mezzanine finance is not a substitute for equity. Because it carries a higher interest rate than senior debt, it represents a higher fixed burden for the borrower. Its use is appropriate, therefore, to finance companies which enjoy stable earnings and a strong cashflow, but which do not have sufficient assets to secure their entire borrowing requirement as senior debt.

An increasing number of banks are prepared to provide senior debt on the basis of an assured future cashflow instead of physical security, ('cashflow lending') and you should fully explore the extent of senior debt available before pursuing mezzanine financing.

The equity deal

In Chapter One we looked at the investor's requirement for a capital gain, the basic elements of the equity split between the management team of Plunder and the investor and the use of Preference Shares to increase the management's percentage holding of the company while slightly reducing the risk to the investor.

This approach forms the basis of most unquoted investment structures. We will now look at some of the refinements used to tailor an investment structure to the requirements of the investor and the company.

Running yield

In the example in Chapter One, all of the investor's return arose from a capital gain on the sale of his Ordinary shares. During the four-year life of the investment, he received not a penny. Although this sounds true to the ideal of long-term equity investing in the purest sense, it has a number of drawbacks for the venture capital company. The investor will have overheads and salaries or management fees to pay, and would ideally like to be able to show a profit on a year-to-year basis, not simply to wait for all of his return years into the future. Also, by taking all of his return from a share of the proceeds in the sale of the company, he is reducing the share of the equity available for its managers. If the investor took some of his return by way of dividends or interest payments during the life of his investment, he would need less of a capital gain when the company was sold, leaving a greater proportion for the management.

It is therefore common to incorporate a running yield—a continuous stream of dividends to the investor—in an investment structure. It is important that this running yield must not place a fixed financial burden on the company, undoing all the good that adopting a conservative level of debt financing has done.

The use of dividends has the advantage in this respect that a dividend can only be paid out of retained profits. From the tax point of view, of course, dividends are extremely inefficient as they are paid out of the company's after tax profits, and have the cashflow disadvantage of requiring Advance Corporation Tax payments to be made.

Running yield can be broken down into two forms—Fixed and Participating Yield.

A *fixed yield* is simply a level of dividend, on either Ordinary or Preference shares, fixed at a certain percentage of the cost to the investors of those shares. Typically, the fixed dividend will run at something between 7.5 and 12 per cent pa, and be payable semi-annually. Companies not showing strongly profitable trading at the time of the investment will generally negotiate a 'dividend holiday', during which dividends will not be payable.

Preference shares almost always carry a fixed yield, whereas the practice with Ordinary shares varies from investor to investor.

If Ordinary shares held by investors are to carry a yield—or indeed any special right for the investor—they will be designated as a slightly different class (normally 'A' Ordinary shares) to differentiate them from plain Ordinary shares held by the management. They will be convertible into Ordinaries at the investor's option (normally at the time when the company is sold or floated).

A fixed dividend is usually cumulative—if you miss a payment because of inadequate levels of retained profits, it has to be made up once sufficient profits have been achieved. Most investment agreements carry provisions entitling the investor to extra voting rights if the Preference dividends are more than a certain period—normally six months—overdue. On the face of it, this sounds as potentially dangerous as the bank's right to appoint a Receiver. However, unlike a bank which in difficult times may be forced to act to the detriment of shareholders in order to realise its security, the investor will only recover his money if the company returns to profitable trading. His interest, therefore, is solely in ensuring that the best management team is in control. These extra voting rights are dangerous only to the extent that the investor loses faith in you as a management team.

When presenting an investment structure to you, investors will generally quote a yield net of its associated tax credits—in other words you have to pay ACT in addition to the dividend at the rate quoted. See Example 3 (p. 127), which demonstrates the effect on Plunder of agreeing to pay a fixed dividend on the investor's Preference shares.

Participating dividends are normally payable on the investor's ordinary shares, and are based on a percentage of profits. Often they will not be payable during the early part of the investment. See Example 4 (p. 128) for a structure which uses participating dividends.

Participating dividends play a more subtle role than fixed dividends in boosting the investor's return. As the company's profits grow, they come to represent increasingly substantial amounts of money and can place a burden on the management, who might prefer to retain the funds to reinvest in the business. This clearly provides something of an incentive for the management to find an exit for the investor. On the other hand, the increasing levels of dividend, coupled with the steady repayment of most of the cost of his investment by the redemption of his Preference shares, compensates the investor if the exit takes longer than he had anticipated.

The next phase in the venture capital industry's development may be the evolution of investments that are not sold to other companies and never go public. One investor may finance a company as a start-up, early expansion or immature management buyout and back it through its growth stages until it achieves steady, consistent profitability, has a strong, fully developed management team and produces a consistent return from a participating dividend. At this stage, a major institution could buy the shareholding from the venture capital investor on the basis of an entitlement to a consistent stream of dividends directly linked to profits.

Participating dividends are generally linked to the company's profits for each year, after allowing for taxation and fixed dividend obligations (the 'Available Profit'). Thus a 'twice covered' dividend would be equivalent to the investor's *pro rata* share (based on his percentage shareholding) of half the available profit (see Example 4). Although the adoption of the 'twice covered' type of wording implies that all shareholders will receive a dividend (so that half the available profit is paid out), in fact management shareholders will normally not be allowed to take a dividend until the investors' Preference shares have all been redeemed.

Management ratchets

We saw in Chapter One the way in which the use of Preference shares protected the bulk of the venture capitalist's investment while maximising the management's equity holding. The use of a ratchet is a further step down the same path—this time, the idea is to increase the chances of the investor achieving his target return, while enabling the management to increase their share of the equity if the company meets or exceeds the results projected in its business plan.

The basic principle is that, subject to achieving certain levels of performance, a portion of the equity passes from the investor to the management. This is generally done by cancelling some of the Ordinary shares held by the investor, or reducing the number of Ordinary shares into which the investors 'A' Ordinary shares can convert. There are also ratchet structures which work the other way—equity passes from the management to the investors unless certain targets are met—but these are rare.

Ratchet targets can be one, or a combination, of three types:

1. Profits, either for a particular year or over a period of two or three years. This latter approach is clearly fairer to both management and investor, as profits for any one year can be distorted by non-recurring influences. An aggregate profit target over a three-

year period, coupled with a minimum to be achieved each year, is the most demanding basis for consistent performance.

2. Exit valuation. This is the nearest an investor can get to guaranteeing his return, as the increase in management equity is directly linked to the value and time at which a cash exit is achieved, and this type of ratchet target will generally incorporate a time window (typically two or three years) with a schedule of exit valuation targets which increase each year. Example 5 (p. 129) shows a ratchet structure incorporating an exit target applied to our fictional (and versatile!) management buyout.

3. Cash return. Typically linked to early redemption of Preference shares. This is the least common form of ratchet target, and is used when a management team projects that they only need funding for a short period of time, but for a project which presents an equity level of risk. Typical examples might be a management buyout where a division or subsidiary could be sold off quickly, or financing for an acquisition which after a bedding-down period could be refinanced by bank debt.

At first sight, a ratchet does appear to be the ideal answer to those tricky negotiations when management and investor cannot agree on a set of investment terms. If the company underperforms, then the investor's return is, to some extent at least, protected by a larger percentage shareholding, while if the management team achieve all they promise they will be rewarded by a greater share of the company. However practice has shown some distinct drawbacks.

Arbitrary objectives

If you have ever set a bonus scheme for a sales force, you will know this problem. No matter how closely you attempt to set the rules to match the company's long-term interest, you end up with a set of arbitrary targets which the sales force will pursue for their own sake. The same is true of a set of ratchet targets. The relatively simplistic objectives may cause you to pursue short-term profits at the expense of long-term growth, sell the company before its value is maximised in order to meet the constraint of an exit ratchet or replace low yielding Preference shares with expensive debt in order to meet a money back target.

Risk/Reward distortion

If, because of a ratchet, the investor will not receive the full benefit of the rapid expansion of your business, he is less likely to accept the risk such an expansion would entail. The ratchet is divisive—it creates a conflict of interest between management and investor, because their rewards are not linked in the same way to the success of the company.

Distortion of investor's return

There is no reason for you to feel sympathetic to this point, but you should understand it. The overall return on a portfolio of unquoted investments does not arise, in practice, from consistent returns by all or most of the investments. It comes from higher than average performance from some, which balances low returns, failures to exit and outright losses on others. A ratchet distorts this balance by to some extent limiting, or reducing, the return on the successful investments.

Over-leverage of management position

As we have seen, the use of preference shares means that the amount of money the management makes when the business is sold is not simply a linear function of the sale price . The use of a ratchet exacerbates this effect. This means that, should the company fall short of its targets, then not only will it be worth less than the management envisaged but they will have a smaller share. As Example 5 demonstrates, the effects of this can be significant enough to demotivate the team completely.

Complication of subsequent rounds

A straw poll of venture capital executives reveals that the share structure of an unquoted company is rarely left alone long enough for the terms of a ratchet to be fully worked out. Typically, either the company needs further funding, an acquisition opportunity or a significant change of strategic direction occurs first—in sum, the assumptions which drove the ratchet structure no longer hold good. The existence of a ratchet mechanism adds a significant layer of complication to the negotiations attached to any further financing.

How much do the management need to invest?

In summary, enough to represent a major personal financial commitment. The management investment need not be a significant amount in the context of the overall financing, but should represent 'hurt money'—an amount large enough to ensure that each member of the team will not be prepared to walk away from the company and write it off should the going become difficult.

The bulk of individual management investments fall in the region of £30,000 to £60,000, usually funded by a second mortgage.

The question of a cash management investment generally only arises for management buyouts or buyins or for start-ups. In the case of an existing company seeking expansion financing, the investor is, normally, unlikely to wish to see further investment from the management. The major exception to this would be for an early stage or other high-risk proposition where the management has not ever made a significant personal investment.

Early stage companies

We have used a development capital investment as the basis for our examples, because it permitted the exploration of a variety of techniques. The structures shown are equally applicable to Plunder as a management buyout, buyin or expansion financing. However, for those contemplating raising funds for a start-up or young company, there are a number of additional considerations.

Uncertainty

The major factor which, from the investment structuring viewpoint, differentiates early stage companies is the higher degree of uncertainty about future levels of revenues (and even costs). This, together with the fact that the company generally has little in the way of assets to offer a bank as security, requires that the bulk of financing at this stage will be by way of equity.

The other consequence is uncertainty about the amount of financing required. The need to be adequately funded on the one hand is in conflict with the desire to raise as little external capital, and so retain as much equity as possible, on the other. It is difficult to make generalised comments, but I cannot resist mentioning that I have been involved in financing small companies for some ten years and have yet to see one that raised too much equity.

The solution is to raise money in a number of stages, with each round linked to the achievement of a specific objective. For example, starting from scratch, a company might seek separate rounds for each of the following milestones, over say a seven-year period:

- Product development and market research.

- Product launch, initial marketing and proof of concept.

- Major marketing offensive, turnover growth to break even level.

- Working capital for continued revenue growth.

- Finance for geographic and product diversification.

This approach has a number of advantages over the attempt, which we see fail so often, to raise enough funding for a start-up to take it right the way through to a float or sale. The advantages are that the amount of finance required can be assessed more accurately, and overall, funding will be raised on better terms because each successive round will be more attractive to investors (rather than raising all of the funding at the outset, when the entire investment will be negotiated on start-up terms). Furthermore, it is easier to persuade an investor that a specific stage can be reached in, say two to three years, rather than a more general target in seven, although the investor does, of course, have to believe the business will have continuing merit.

Raising finance by stages is more flexible; if it becomes clear after the market research stage, for example, that the product can only be marketed by a major global corporation then a corporate, rather than a financial partner can be sought.

Negotiations

The chances are that you will be in a weaker position when negotiating terms, as there will be a smaller universe of potential investors to compete with each other. The following are some important points to bear in mind when negotiating finance.

- Cater for as wide a range of outcomes as possible; you might end up building a quoted giant or you might decide to license your product after a year and go off to invent something else. Ensure that the terms of the funding suit you across the range of likely eventualities.

- The general approach of the investor, even more so than when financing a stronger, established company, is more important than minor differences in the terms. To an even greater extent than in a development capital financing you are choosing a partner, not simply a source of funds, and the choice of that partner will significantly influence your success.

- Bear in mind that you will almost certainly need to raise further rounds of funding, and do not agree to any structures which are so complicated as to make this difficult. Discuss with the investor his likely role in and contribution to further funding.

Example 1a: The starting point

We left the management team of Plunder in Chapter One, having arranged a basic Ordinary share, Preference share and medium term loan financing for their management buyout. As a reminder, it looked like this:

Financing Requirement	£	
Fixed Asset Acquisition	2,500,000	
Legal, etc. Expenses	100,000	
	2,600,000	

Funded by:

£1 Ordinary Shares (at par)

Management	100,000	41%
Investors	144,000	59%
Preference Shares	856,000	
TOTAL EQUITY FINANCING	1,100,000	
Medium Term Loan (@ 15%)	1,500,000	
	2,600,000	

The team had also arranged a £1m overdraft facility, to cover the working capital requirements and the need to purchase £250,000 of stock at the time of the buyout. The projected Profit and Loss Account looks as follows:

£000s

Year to 31 December	1991	1992	1993	1994
Turnover	4,700	5,640	6,768	8,122
Gross Profit	1,128	1,410	1,692	2,030
Less:				
Overheads	550	605	666	732
Profit Before Interest and Tax (PBIT)	578	805	1,027	1,298
Less:				
Medium Term Loan Interest	225	191	146	101
Overdraft Interest	80	123	108	60
Profit Before Tax	273	491	772	1,137
Less:				
Notional Tax (35%)	95	172	270	398
Profit Retained	177	319	502	739

The investors and management anticipate selling the company in December 1994 at a PE Ratio of 8 on its Profit after Tax of £739,375 for that year, giving a sale price of £5,915,000.

This is parcelled out to the shareholders as follows:

	£000s
Sale Proceeds	5,915
Preference Share Redemption	856
Available For Ordinary Shareholders	5,059
Management	2,073
Investor	2,986

The investor receives a total return of £3,842,000 on 31 December 1994. This represents an annual compound growth rate (or Internal Rate of Return, shortened to 'IRR') of 40 per cent on his investment of £1,000,000 on 1 January 1991.

Example 1b: Leverage

While negotiating the finer points of the deal with the venture capitalists, Plunder's management team is approached by a banker, hungry for business, who feels that the assets they are buying for £2.5 m represent adequate security for a £2 m loan. This would halve the amount of external equity the team needs to raise, to £500,000, enabling them to retain a greater share of the business.

The revised forecast Profit and Loss Account, with allowances for extra interest, is as follows:

£000s

Year to 31 December	*1991*	*1992*	*1993*	*1994*
PBIT (as before)	578	805	1,027	1,298
Less:				
Medium Term Loan Interest	300	255	195	135
Overdraft Interest	90	156	167	144
Profit Before Tax	188	394	665	1,019

As with Example 1a, the medium term loan is repayable in ten six monthly tranches, the first on 31 December 1992. Note that not only are the loan interest charges now higher because of the extra borrowings, but so are those for the overdraft, as the debt service requirements drain more cash from the company.

The clear advantage of adopting this level of debt is the amount of equity the management team can retain. In order to earn a 40 per cent pa compound return on a £500,000 investment, based on these forecasts, an external investor will now require only 30 per cent of the equity (42,500 £1 Ordinary shares, 457,500 Preference shares). This leaves 70 per cent for the management team, compared with the 41 per cent they retained in Example 1a.

This improvement is a natural consequence of raising an additional £500,000 at a cost of 15 per cent pa, rather than the 40 per cent sought by equity investors. There is a cost however, which is the increase in the fixed burden on the company.

For the first year after the buyout, Plunder projects PBIT of £578,000, which is only £188,000 more than the anticipated interest charge. A reduction of that amount in the gross profit for the year—equivalent to a fall of £752,000 or 16 per cent in sales revenue—would put Plunder into a loss for the year.

On the original structure, with £1,500,000 medium term loan, PBIT exceeds total interest charges by £273,000, implying room for a 23 per cent shortfall in sales before a failure to meet the interest bill. A comparison of the interest cover ratios for Plunder under the two structures summarises the difference:

Interest Cover (PBIT/Total Interest Charge):

Year to 31 December	*1991*	*1992*	*1993*	*1994*
Example 1a	1.89	2.56	4.03	8.07
Example 1b	1.48	1.96	2.84	4.65

One consequence of the increased level of risk which adoption of this structure entails will be the demand for a higher return for the equity investor, as the chances of him losing his investment are increased. Thus the management team would not receive all of the benefit in increased equity detailed above.

Example 2: Mezzanine

Plunder's management has become excited at the prospect of owning 70 per cent of the company after the buyout, and is sufficiently confident of the financial projections to accept the higher levels of risk associated with a more leveraged buyout. Unfortunately, the bank does not share the team's faith and, after a closer review of the assets available as security decides that a loan of £1.5 m is, after all, as far as it is prepared to go.

The team's disappointment is shortlived as, hot on the trail of interest only funding, it unearths a mezzanine lender. The provider of mezzanine debt is willing to accept a lower level of security for his loan, in exchange for a greater reward, provided that he is confident that the borrower will generate sufficient profits and cashflow to meet his interest and principal repayments. Plunder's management persuades him that a large portion of the company's forecast revenue comes from a number of longstanding, long-term contracts and thus carries a high degree of certainty.

The mezzanine lender offers a £750,000 loan, repayable in eight semi-annual instalments commencing June 1994, with an 18 per cent pa interest rate. This is in addition to the £1,500,000 medium term loan offered by the bank, which will rank ahead of the mezzanine loan as a claimant on the assets of the company as security and is therefore referred to as a senior loan. Note also that repayments of the mezzanine loan do not commence until June 1994, by which time a substantial part of the senior loan will have been repaid.

By borrowing a further £750,000, the team has reduced the external equity requirement from £1,000,000 to £250,000. The effect of carrying interest on that additional loan is as follows:

£000s				
Year to 31 December	*1991*	*1992*	*1993*	*1994*
PBIT (as before)	578	805	1,027	1,298
Less:				
Medium Term Loan Interest	225	191	146	101
Overdraft Interest	91	153	157	188
Mezzanine Interest	135	135	135	127

Profit Before Tax	127	325	588	882

Interest Cover (PBIT/Total Interest Charge):

Year to 31 December	*1991*	*1992*	*1993*	*1994*
Example 1a	1.89	2.56	4.03	8.07
Example 2	1.28	1.68	2.34	3.12

The burden of fixed commitments on the company is now becoming excessive. The mezzanine lender will not be content with an 18 per cent pa return, given the level of risk he is facing. He will require options to purchase Ordinary shares, at a nominal price, representing 7.6 per cent of the company's equity. This will bring his overall rate of return up to 27 per cent pa, assuming the company is sold at December 1994 for 8 times its after tax earnings for that year. On the same assumption, the external equity investor will require 16.7 per cent of the company in order to achieve an IRR of 40 per cent pa on his investment, leaving 75.8 per cent of the equity for the management.

Example 3: Fixed yield

Negotiations with the lenders continue until, one morning, two major customers telephone with complaints about the level of service they have been receiving from Plunder recently. These are simply a function of the attention the management team has been paying to structuring the buyout and are soon put right. However the calls serve the purpose of reminding the team that future revenues are never guaranteed.

Reluctantly, the team decide that the levels of borrowing they had been contemplating entail too much risk, and revert to the original financing structure.

However, they wonder whether they can increase their shareholding to some extent by having the equity investor take some of his return from the company itself during the life of the investment. The investor proposes a fixed dividend of 10 per cent pa on his Preference shares. By earning a 10 per cent pa return on most of his money throughout the life of the investment, he can reduce the IRR he needs to realise from a capital gain to a little over 30 per cent.

Thus the investment structure is now as follows:

£1 Ordinary Shares (at par)

Management	100,000	52.6%

Investors	90,000	47.4%

10% Cumulative Redeemable Preference Shares

Investors	910,000

The investor has subscribed a smaller proportion of his money for Ordinary shares, as he now requires a lesser share of the company's equity.

The company will now be obliged, provided its level of retained profit is sufficient, to pay £91,000 a year to the investors (usually in semi-annual instalments), and also to make the associated Advance Corporation Tax payment to the Inland Revenue.

The Profit and Loss Account will look as follows:

Profit Before Tax*	265	468	731	1,077
Less:				
Tax (35%)	93	164	256	377
Fixed Dividend	91	91	91	91
Profit Retained	82	213	384	609

*This is almost the same figure as in Example 1a, reduced slightly as interest on the overdraft has increased because the payments of the fixed dividend was funded by increased borrowing.

Example 4: Participating yield

Clearly the more return an investor can take from the Company, the less he needs to take as a capital gain at the time of exit and so the more will be available for the management shareholders. The fixed dividend on the Preference shares outlined in Example 3 is about as far as it is reasonable to go in terms of placing a fixed obligation on Plunder; any further running yield will have to be dependent upon the company's performance. The next stage, therefore, is to entitle the investor to a proportion of Plunder's profits each year, after allowing for tax and fixed dividend obligations.

The investor proposes a 'twice covered' dividend; in other words, half the available profit would be earmarked for distribution (the dividend payment is twice covered by the available profit). However only the investors will actually receive their share of this; management share-holders are, in general, not entitled to take a dividend until the bulk of the investor's Preference shares have been redeemed.

By taking a further part of its return in this manner, the investor is able further to reduce its share of the equity, to 41.2 per cent. The share structure is now as follows:

£1 Ordinary Shares (at par)

Management	100,000	58.8%
*Investors**	70,000	41.2%

*These will now be designated 'A' Ordinary shares, in order to differentiate them from the management Ordinary Shares which do not carry the entitlement to a participating dividend.

10% Cumulative Redeemable Preference Shares

Investors	930,000

The Profit and Loss Account will look as follows:

Profit Before Tax	264	461	714	1,041
Less:				
Tax (35%)	92	161	250	364
Fixed Dividend	93	93	93	93
Available Profit	79	207	371	584
Participating Dividend*	16	43	76	120
Profit Retained	63	213	384	609

*41.2% of half the available profit.

Example 5: Management ratchet

The final manifestation of the management's determination to own as much of the equity as possible is the negotiation of a ratchet. As out-lined in the text, ratchet targets can be based on profits, exit valuations or return of cash to investors. Investors generally prefer exit valuation targets, as they motivate the management to achieve an exit and adjust the relative equity holdings by direct reference to the investor's return.

In the case of Plunder, it is agreed that a ratchet based on a sale of the company by 31 December 1994 will be adopted. The investor will initially purchase 'A' Ordinary shares, giving it 46 per cent of the equity. These 'A' Ordinary shares will convert into a number of Ordinary shares at the time of exit, in order to give the investors an equity percentage based on the following table:

	£000s			
Company Sale Price	5,000	6,000	7,000	8,000
Investor's Equity	46.0%	42.7%	39.3%	36.0%

The maximum equity holding for the investor is 46 per cent. If the company is sold for less than £5 m, or is not sold at all before 31 December 1994, the investor's 'A' Ordinary shares convert on a one-for-one basis. If the company is sold for more than £8 m, the investor's share is not reduced below 36 per cent.

UNDER THE MICROSCOPE

The investor's due diligence process

You have sold your proposal to a venture capital company. An investor believes in you and your story, and you have agreed the outline of the terms on which he will provide equity financing.

It has been a wearying process, from the development of the business plan through the series of cold calls to advisers and venture capital companies, the endless repetition of the same story to critical, uninformed financiers, the rewarding flickers of interest and the haggling over a set of investment terms. But now an outline deal is agreed and all is over bar the shouting.

Unfortunately not. Every approval and agreement you have from an investor up to now is subject to his 'Due Diligence' process. You may very well have an offer letter at this stage—or at least a letter which the venture capital executive will describe as an offer letter, but a close inspection of the preamble will reveal it as no more than an outline of the terms on which the investor will be prepared to provide finance once the due diligence is completed.

What is due diligence?

It is the professional care and attention—the diligence—that is due from the venture capital company to those whose money it manages. It represents the difference between an individual backing hunches and a professional fund manager making considered, professional investment decisions based on a clear process and a logical trail of thought. At least, so runs the theory.

When does due diligence start?

Venture capital companies vary in the way the deal-making process is organised. In general, the early appraisal and structuring of investment terms will be based on the venture capitalist forming a fairly subjective view of your management team's calibre, taking the factual elements of your business plan and financials at face value and using his and his colleagues' experience to analyse your strategic thinking. The investor will usually want to discuss outline terms with you at this early stage, if only to ensure that he is not wasting time pursuing a proposal on which there is no hope of agreeing terms.

This approach is far from universal, and some venture capitalists will, particularly with early stage investments, not even begin to discuss terms until they have fully investigated the proposal. However, the increasing competition for opportunities to invest in established companies means that most venture houses will attempt to secure a deal by taking the 'Face Value' approach, negotiating outline terms and reaching an agreement—in principle and subject to formal due diligence—with the entrepreneur or management team reasonably quickly.

The larger and lower risk the transaction—which means increased competition among the investors and a higher reliance by them on financial structuring to secure and profit from a proposal—the more likely you are to receive an early indication of terms from an investor. At the other end of the scale, expect a venture house to spend many weeks poring over your start-up before even beginning to talk seriously about terms.

What does it consist of?

The elements of the due diligence process are:

- factual verification of the company's trading history, and statements of fact in the business plan;

- management review;

- product and technical appraisal;

- independent market review;

- references;

- accountant's investigation.

Factual verification

The investor will want to check out the factual statements contained in your business plan. You can accelerate this part of the process by providing:

- audited accounts;

- copies of any market research or report material upon which parts of the plan are based;

- relevant press and industry comment, articles or reviews;

- copies of important contracts or other significant legal agreements;

- published accounts of competitors, if you have them;

- your Memorandum and Articles of Association.

Management review

This is a detailed review of the management structure of your company, with emphasis on:

- its adequacy;

- the competence of the management;

- requirements for the future;

- succession;

- quality of junior management;

- personal objectives of each member of the team.

It may be conducted by an executive of the venture capital house or by an outside consultant.

Be prepared to provide full job descriptions for each of your key personnel, and to explain in some depth how the management structure functions in practice as well as on paper.

Product or service and technical appraisal

This aspect will assume more importance in early stage companies. If you are raising finance for a start up or very young company whose business plan is built around a narrow range of products or services, expect the investor to commission a detailed product review, while for a more established company with a broader range of activities this part of the due diligence process will receive less attention.

If your plan entails an element of product development, then this stage of the due diligence will incorporate a review of the prospects for its successful completion.

Independent market review

It would be a foolish investor who based his appraisal of a company's market solely on the views of the company's management team. Expect the venture capitalist to seek an objective view, either by undertaking research himself or by commissioning a consultant's report.

He will be seeking to confirm the assumptions and summaries about the market on which your strategy and business case are based, and which he probably took at face value when working up an investment proposal. After the quality of a company's management, its market will be regarded as the most critical factor in the success or failure of the investment and you can expect a great deal of attention to be paid to this area. The investor will be concerned not only with the size and growth prospects of your market, but with its shape and structure. He will be seeking to deepen his understanding of how your company fits into the market and how your strategy will work.

References

The investor will want references of two types; on the company and on the management team. References are an important source of outside confirmation that the company and its management team can perform the functions required to meet the business plan.

Reference taking is a sensitive area, and the venture capitalist will not undertake this until he is fairly sure that the investment is likely to reach completion. He will probably ask you to warn the referees that he will be contacting them, and will not do so until you authorise him. Investors generally use a combination of telephone calls and letters to take references.

A typical telephone call or letter might ask the following questions of a referee:

- How long have you known/been trading with [subject]?
- What is the nature of your relationship?

  personal; professional; customer; supplier.

The venture capitalist will choose his questions and view the responses to them in the light of the relationship.

- What is the extent of the business relationship? (turnover, importance of subject as supplier/customer)
- What are your views of [subject]'s service/product?

- How do you view the market for [subject]'s services or product?

- How much do you know about [subject]'s market positioning and strategy (and if appropriate) what are your views on these areas?

- How do you rate [subject]'s management?

- How does [subject] compare to its competitors?

- Are there any other factors which you think we should bear in mind when making an investment decision?

A number of entrepreneurs and management teams become understandably nervous at the prospect of having some ham-fisted financier ringing up their most precious business contacts and asking impertinent questions. However I have never known this part of the process to do a company any harm—most of the hundreds of referees I have spoken to have been encouraged to hear that their trading partners are being strengthened by an equity injection.

The accountant's investigation

The investor will almost certainly instruct an accountancy firm to review the financial elements of your business plan and trading history. He will ask them to report to him about the following.

Historic results

The accountant will often review your auditor's papers and give an opinion on:

- the basis on which accounts were prepared;

- the extent to which the accounts present a true and fair view of your company's performance;

- verification of principal assets;

- any major influences on your historic results of which an investor should be aware;

- confirmation that there are no hidden actual or contingent liabilities (litigation, taxation, etc.)

- historic performance against budgets.

Management accounts and systems

The investigation will review:

- the quality of your management accounting systems;

- the completeness and accuracy of the management information produced;

- adequacy of internal control systems;

- the extent and quality of your budgeting process;

- current year to date performance against budget.

Financial forecasts

The accountant will analyse your projections to ensure that:

- the numbers add up;

- they have been prepared on the assumptions and bases that you outlined in your business plan;

- any inconsistencies with historic performance are explained.

Some venture capitalists ask the accountant for an opinion on the achievability of the forecasts.

How to approach due diligence

It is important—and sometimes difficult—to remember that by the time he decides to undertake detailed due diligence, the venture capitalist is well on the way to deciding that he wants to invest in your company.

You have climbed most of the uphill slope, in convincing him that your business and its management are strong enough to back. In a sense, the process is now negative—he is making sure that the facts, opinions and assumptions on which he based his decisions are true or reasonable, and there are no significant other facts or influences which would affect his decision to invest.

After you have reached an outline agreement on an investment, insist that the venture capitalist outlines the due diligence work he needs to do, explaining the rationale for each part of the process and indicating the timetable to which he expects to work.

You can help make the due diligence process easy for the investor by anticipating his needs, providing him with information where appropriate or directing him to its source. Put yourself in the shoes of the investor—

what are the principal assumptions on which he has decided to invest, what will he see as the major areas of risk and what would you need to support the investment decision had you made it? By staying a step ahead, you can be prepared to meet his needs, making his job easier and accelerating the process.

Stay in touch with the venture capitalist during this phase. By doing so you will receive continuing feedback on his progress, at the same time ensuring that his attention remains focused on your proposal.

Further negotiations

During the due diligence stage, an investor will normally only pull out of a transaction if he comes across some fundamental problem that demolishes the basis on which his decision to invest was taken. For example:

- A serious flaw in the management team becomes apparent;

- The independent market review reveals a totally different picture from that presented in your business plan;

- The product or service does not work;

- A high proportion of referees provide serious negative comments, about either the business or the management team;

- The financial projections are hopelessly unrealistic.

Remember that the investor now has a great deal of work invested in the proposition and, more significantly, has seen a management team and a business concept which he finds attractive. He is unlikely to let go lightly.

A more common happening is for the venture capitalist to form a slightly different view of the opportunity, the business or the management. He might talk to a consultant who anticipates a different rate of market growth, for example, or a couple of your customers acting as referees might point out that you are losing market share because your product or service is lacking a certain element. This can have two effects.

The first is that the venture capitalist will explore these problems or inconsistencies with you. This is a valuable exercise for both parties—he gains extra insight into your business, while you are provided with further opportunities to impress him with the depth of your industry knowledge and the foresight of your planning.

The other effect is that he may wish, if he discovers factors which have a material impact on your likely performance or the risk he is taking, to adjust the terms of the investment. It is quite common for the amount of funding to be increased at this stage, as the investor comes to the view, with which he persuades a management team to concur, that success is in fact a peak hidden behind the one on the business plan.

Of course, he won't adjust the terms in your favour: to do so would be a reflection of a failure on your part to sell the proposal properly in the first place, as the venture capitalist would have found further positive aspects to which you had not drawn his attention.

You are, at this stage, perfectly free to withdraw and reopen negotiations with one of the other investors you had been talking to. However, before doing so, think carefully about the reasons for the venture capitalist's desire to revisit the terms. He will not have proposed a change without good reason, as it creates the risk of generating a difficult relationship with you and possibly losing the opportunity to invest. If he has come across factors significant enough to make him take that risk, it is quite likely that the next investor you talk to will take the same view. So before tearing up the agreement and starting afresh, ask yourself is the venture capitalist simply trying to extort better terms out of me on the basis of some fictitious shortcomings in my business because he thinks I have nowhere else to go, or is he forming a completely irrational conclusion about the proposal, based on misleading information and his own faulty understanding of my industry?

If the answer to both of those questions is no, then your best interests will probably be served by negotiating a new set of terms, rather than calling a halt and seeking a new investor. You do, however, have nothing to lose by playing tough at this stage. The venture capitalist will be reluctant to lose the deal and will be sensitive to the relationship problems which a renegotiation at this stage can cause (although they are only a reflection of his doing the job properly).

Turn the tables

The due diligence phase of the investment process gives you the opportunity to learn more about your potential financial partner. If you have not yet spoken to some of his existing investee companies, take the time to do so now.

Also, the way the deal is driven through the detailed investigation process will tell you a great deal about both the executives you are working with and the house they represent. Look for a focus on the major commercial issues which lie behind their investment decision, a constructive approach to solving problems or resolving conflicts which emerge from the process and a willingness to move the due diligence at a reasonable pace so that the investment can be completed. An unfocused approach to the due diligence, a tendency to become waylaid and overly concerned by details and lack of clear progress through the process are causes for concern. Remember that these people will become partners in your business.

Final approval and the offer letter

At last, you will have satisfied the investor's final commercial requirements and he will obtain, from his investment committee or similar body, final approval to invest subject only to satisfactory documentation. The deal goes into legal stages.

The next chapter reviews the legal process and the various documents which you will need to agree and sign. However there are a number of areas which should be agreed between you and the investor before the legal process starts. Negotiating commercial points, unfamiliar to you, raised unexpectedly by the venture capitalist, under the pressure of a legal completion deadline and with phalanxes of expensive professionals around the table is not the basis for a constructive start to your relationship with an investor.

Therefore, in addition to the purely financial details covered in Chapter Six, you should agree with the investor—and the agreement should be incorporated in the offer letter—on the following areas:

- Conditions precedent

Exactly what has to happen before the investment is completed?

- Investor director

Will the investor appoint a director to your board? (Chapter Nine looks at this area in detail.) If so, how often are board meetings to be held and what are his fees to be?

- Future transactions

As you will read in the next chapter, the documentation will contain undertakings from you designed to ensure, in essence, that you keep, as far as possible, to the business plan on which the investment is made. These undertakings will cover areas such as levels of capital expenditure, hiring of senior personnel, acquisition or disposal of subsidiaries and major changes in activities. Many venture capitalists' formal offer letters summarise the kind of control they will expect in this area—ensure that you understand and are comfortable with the extent of the restrictions the investor intends to place on you.

- Directors' warranties

You will be required by the investor to warrant that certain facts are true and that you have not misled him in any way. These warranties will be negotiated in detail with your lawyers present. However it is worth while at this stage asking the investor about his approach to this area. Some will insist on detailed, wide-ranging warranties, while others are content with some general statements that you have been accurate and not misleading in the information you have provided. Knowing the investor's approach before entering the legal negotiation can make the process smoother and reduce the lawyers' fees.

8

SHARKS IN THE WATER

The legal process

by

Mark Aspery, Partner, Cameron Markby Hewitt

The term 'sharks' in the title of this chapter refers, perhaps unfairly, to the lawyers. Their arrival *en masse* will mark the commencement of legal stages, although the management team's own lawyer will usually have been involved during the earlier stages.

As Chapter One mentioned the 'legals' are tedious but essential; tedious because they consist of writing down in legal language virtually everything which has been discussed and agreed since negotiations commenced, essential primarily because the process of documenting the deal serves to highlight any areas where the parties have been at cross-purposes or have still to flesh out the agreed outline terms. Legal stages can also be frustrating in that they reopen questions which everyone assumed had been settled and occasionally throw up substantial problems which require changes to the basic commercial terms previously agreed.

When all goes well with the investment, the voluminous legal documentation which results from legal stages will rarely be referred to after completion. However if things go awry each of the interested parties will grab their 'bible' of legal documents in the expectation that it will contain the solutions to at least some of their problems.

This chapter will give you an idea of what to expect from the legal process and from the lawyers themselves. It reviews a management buyout, simply because this is the most involved of all the transaction types and enables us to cover every aspect of the legal process. All of the documents and processes described here will be relevant for a buyout, a buyin or an acquisition financing; those which relate to the acquisition of a company will clearly be irrelevant for an expansion or start-up investment.

Before considering the different types of document involved and the purposes they are intended to serve it is worth listing the different breeds of shark which you will encounter and considering the roles which they each play.

The management team's lawyer

Your own legal adviser plays the key role. He has to deal with the lawyers for the venture capitalist and bankers and at the same time negotiate the legal terms of the acquisition with the vendor's lawyers. His involvement in all aspects of the legal work means that he is the obvious person to stage manage the legal stages and to ensure that progress is made on all fronts simultaneously. His main tasks can be summarised as follows:

1. Understand—and probably write down as Heads of Agreement—the terms on which the vendor has agreed to sell the target company. Though the Heads will probably be non-binding they may include binding commitments that

   (a) there will be no negotiations with a view to selling the target to anyone else for an agreed period (usually referred to as a 'lock-out' period) and

   (b) a contribution will be paid towards the costs of the management team in the event that the vendor chooses not to proceed.

2. If necessary, incorporate the new company which will be used to buy the target and attend to its shareholding structure. Your lawyer should offer advice about the most efficient way in which the management team can make their personal investments.

3. Review with the management team the offer letter from the venture capital investor. Although this will invariably be subject to contract (ie non-binding) it is important to negotiate out any unacceptable terms at this stage. Also legal advice on the terms of the offer letter will better enable the team to evaluate the relative merits of different offers received. However, care should be taken not to get too 'bogged down' in the negotiation of the offer letter which (like the Heads of Agreement with the vendor) is only intended to be a broad summary of the principal terms of the investment.

4. Draft the Purchase Contract for submission to the vendor's lawyer having spent time with the management team familiarising himself with the target's business and affairs. Of particular rele-

vance in the case of a buyout is the existing role played by the management team in running the business; this has a bearing on the extent to which the vendor can legitimately refuse to give detailed confirmations concerning aspects of the business within the management's knowledge.

5. Prepare Service Contracts to be entered into between the company and each member of the team. This is one of a number of areas where your lawyer wears several hats in that he has to balance the individual requirements of members of the team for generous remuneration and benefits and protection from dismissal against the requirement that the company (in the shape of its shareholders collectively) has the normal rights of an employer. The contracts must also be in a form acceptable to the investor.

6. Negotiate the investment documents with the venture capitalist's lawyer and produce a 'Disclosure Letter' (see the section on the Investment Agreement below).

7. Negotiate the loan documents with the bank's lawyer. These will be of varying complexity depending on the sophistication of the loan facilities which have been negotiated.

Thus far it has been assumed that the management team's lawyer will be a single individual but in reality your legal advice is likely to be provided by a team of lawyers. Where necessary the lawyers instructed by you should be prepared to field a number of individuals to concentrate on specific aspects of the job and you should ensure that the firm concerned has adequate in-house expertise both in dealing with venture capital backed deals and on relevant specific subjects such as taxation, real property, pensions, trade marks, patents and so on.

Other lawyers

There may be up to half a dozen lawyers 'on the other side' since the vendor, each venture capitalist, each bank and any mezzanine financier will probably wish to be separately represented. In one way or another the fees of all these lawyers will be paid by the company and it is well worth considering at the outset whether the number of players (and so the costs) can be reduced by getting a syndicate of investors to agree that they will all instruct the same lawyer.

Although the management team's own lawyer will 'shield' his clients from the other lawyers involved, the face to face meeting with lawyers and clients to thrash out the legal documents is almost inevitable and it is as well to have some appreciation of the primary concerns of the lawyers involved.

The vendor's lawyer

It is difficult to generalise about the vendor's lawyer since this will depend on the nature of the vendor or vendors. If you are buying out a division of a large quoted company, the vendor is likely to instruct a firm of lawyers which is well used to dealing with corporate mergers and acquisitions work. If the vendors are individuals, there is a danger that the vendors will instruct a lawyer with little experience of corporate deals or lacking the resources to deal with the matter against a tight timetable. As a general rule, it is of benefit for all of the parties if the vendor chooses a lawyer with specific experience of corporate transactions.

Your own lawyer will draw up the contract for the acquisition and it is the vendor's lawyer's job to cross out as much of this as possible. His approach will be that his client expects to receive an agreed purchase price with the minimum of legal complications and does not wish to allow the company any 'come-back' if problems arise after the deal is done. On the other hand, the vendor's lawyer has to realise that the management team (and more particularly their financial backers) have exactly the opposite as their objective and that ultimately the purchase price will not be available unless the contract contains adequate safe-guards.

The venture capitalist's lawyer

The venture capitalist's lawyer will almost certainly be experienced in this type of transaction and, in a well run deal, can be of considerable assistance to the management team. While he is clearly the 'opposition' when it comes to negotiating the investment documents, he is very much on your side when it comes to dealing with the lawyers who represent the vendor and the providers of loan finance. This is because as shareholders in the company the management team and the venture capitalist are equally interested in acquiring the target business and obtaining loan finance on the most favourable terms. In fact, the venture capitalist's lawyer is sometimes given the entire responsibility for dealing on behalf of the company with the acquisition and the loan finance. Where this happens the role of the management team's lawyer is restricted to negotiation of the equity investment documents and the preparation of the service contracts.

The lender's lawyers

Late in the day, lawyers for the bank and other lenders to the company will make their appearance. The reason for the late start by these lawyers is that the debt element of the financing is only negotiated once terms have been agreed with the venture capitalist. Also it will be part of their task to review the acquisition and equity investment documents in their largely final state. It is not unusual to see the lawyers for the management team and the venture capitalist 'ganging up' against the bank's lawyer when negotiating the loan documentation but often to no avail. The bank's lawyer knows that the deal cannot proceed without his client's money and that, given the time and effort which has already been put in by the remaining parties, there will now be immense pressure to get the deal done. You may come up against a certain rigidity of approach because the bank's lawyers have developed standardised documentation from which they are very reluctant to depart.

In addition to recording the terms on which moneys are to be advanced to the company, the bank's lawyer will be required to secure the bank's loan by taking charges over the assets of the company and of the business to be acquired. In order to do this, he will need to establish (by making official searches and the like) that the target actually owns the assets—in the jargon he will 'investigate title'.

Almost inevitably in a management buyout, the taking of security over the assets of the target company will involve the company giving financial assistance for the acquisition of its shares. Companies legislation now permits the giving of financial assistance but required the parties to jump through various legal hoops before this is done. The bank's lawyer will worry deeply before eventually advising the bank that in this particular case and in these particular circumstances the giving of financial assistance by the target company will not be a criminal offence.

Lawyers generally

At some point during most transactions, the principals could be forgiven for beginning to feel that the lawyers are all narrow-minded and belligerent but this need not be the case. As with the various parties, the primary interest of all the lawyers is to see the transaction brought to a speedy and satisfactory conclusion and any lawyer worth his salt will recognise that this inevitably involves some 'give and take'. All too frequently though, one or other of the lawyers involved will indulge in point scoring with his counterparts or will waste time in arguing legal points which are of little commercial significance. Where the management team detect that this is occurring it may be necessary for them to rein back their own lawyer, or request one of the other parties to do so. It is the role of the lawyers collectively to facilitate the deal and you are entitled to expect them all to approach their task with a constructive attitude and sufficient flexibility to meet the conflicting requirements of all of the parties in the best manner possible.

The legal documentation

If you were surprised by the numbers of lawyers likely to be involved in your transaction, you will be astounded by the volume of paperwork which they are capable of producing. It is probably true to say that the key commercial terms of the transaction could be recorded in documents which are one tenth of the length of those with which you will end up. In the vast majority of cases this would be perfectly adequate. However, the legal documentation looks at what happens when things go wrong:

- How will the company be able to get some of the purchase price back from the vendor?

- How can the company prevent a nervous bank from enforcing its security at a time when there is no real need?

- What will be the position of a member of the management team who is regarded by the investor as under-performing?

- What steps will the equity investor be able to take against the wishes of the management team if it perceives that its investment is in danger?

The legal documents address a host of questions such as these, but in the hope that they will never be asked.

No two deals are the same and legal documents dealing with the same subject matter and having the same purpose can be given different names but, taking the management buyout of Plunder Ltd as an example, the principal documents which are likely to hit your desk are the following:

- Acquisition (or Share Sale) Agreement between the company and the vendor

- Investment (or Subscription) Agreement with the venture capitalist

- Articles of Association recording the rights attaching to the different classes of shares in the company.

- Service Agreements between the individual members of the management team and the company.

- Loan Agreements (or Facility Letters) between the company and its lenders together with associated security documentation.

Acquisition Agreement

This records your deal with the vendor. From your perspective, its primary function is to reverse the legal principle that a buyer of shares has no redress if the target company is not all that it was jacked up to be. This is done by setting out detailed and lengthy statements (known as 'Vendor's Warranties') about the target company, its business, its financial position and (to the extent that you can get away with it) its prospects. These statements are drawn up by the management team's lawyer and in signing the contract the vendor confirms that they are all true and accurate. While your lawyer will be able to produce 50 pages of warranties on subjects as diverse as the accuracy of the latest audited accounts and the state and condition of plant and equipment, it is crucial that the management team alerts him to current problems affecting the business, issues which are of key importance to its future and factors which were instrumental in determining the price to be paid. It is essential that all important aspects are covered by the warranties for two reasons:

1. The Vendor may not be able to make a statement about Plunder without qualifying it and this ensures that the management team and their financial backers go into the deal with their eyes open.

2. There may be a problem relating to Plunder's business which through inadvertence or otherwise is not disclosed by the vendor. If a loss is suffered by the company as a result of matters being not as they were warranted by the vendor, the company may have the legal right to require the vendor to make good the loss.

Special treatment will be afforded to the tax liabilities of Plunder again for two reasons:

1. A corporate group's tax affairs for past accounting periods may not be settled at the time of the sale, but the vendor is nevertheless responsible for all liability to taxation in respect of accounting periods ending before completion.

2.   A change in ownership of Plunder and the fact that it will cease
      to be a member of a corporate group may, of itself, give rise to tax
      charges.

Although the tax is payable by Plunder it is generally accepted that it
should be for the account of the vendor and reimbursed on a pound-
for-pound basis. This commitment will either be included in the Acquisition Agreement itself or in a separate document known as a deed of
indemnity.

The vendor will not take kindly to having words put in its mouth and
will, through its lawyer, seek to amend the warranties or qualify their
effect by making disclosures of specific facts against them. The vendor's
lawyer will also wish to restrict the company's ability to make claims
under the warranties by limiting the total amount which can be claimed,
providing for a monetary threshold which must be reached before any
claims are brought, imposing a time limit and obliging the company to
pursue its rights against third parties before knocking on the vendor's
door. The negotiation of the warranty clause and the limitations which
the vendor wishes to impose are likely to be protracted and the end
result will depend in the main on the bargaining strength of the parties
and their knowledge of Plunder's affairs.

Where the buyout team have sole responsibility for managing the target's business the vendor is likely to refuse to give warranties on the
basis that the team has full knowledge. However, care should be taken
to identify those management functions which are, in fact, dealt with by
the vendor at group level (for example, pensions, tax affairs and supply
arrangements). Remember also that the venture capitalist will look to
the management team to give personal warranties covering any areas on
which comfort was not available from the vendor.

Where there is a management buyin, or any other acquisition of a
business not already known in detail by the management team, it will
prove easier to obtain full warranties from the vendor and, on key
issues, to require the vendor to give absolute confirmations even upon
matters which may be outside its knowledge. Even so, the vendor's lawyer
may seek to minimise the risk to his clients by providing that the vendor
should not be liable in relation to any matter which is within the knowledge of the management team.

The other areas dealt with by the Acquisition Agreement fall into two
more or less distinct parts. The early clauses deal with completion of the
sale and will identify the shares or assets to be sold, the price to be paid
(whether up front or at a later date by reference to, say, future profit)
and the timing of the payments.

Assuming that the buyout of Plunder will result in its leaving a group which consists not only of Pillage but various other fellow subsidiaries, there will inevitably be various intragroup arrangements which need to be unravelled at completion. For example, intragroup trading balances between Plunder and other vendor group companies will need to be paid off and any security given by Plunder to the vendor group bankers will need to be released so that Plunder's assets are available as security for the company's borrowings.

The remainder of the Acquisition Agreement will deal with the ongoing relationship between the vendor and the company and will almost certainly contain restrictions so as to prevent the vendor from establishing a competing business after completion. If Plunder will continue to be dependent on trading arrangements or services provided by the vendor, the Agreement will need to record the terms on which these are to continue.

The Agreement will also record any arrangement for part of the price to be deferred—perhaps subject to the future performance of Plunder—and for outstanding indebtedness of Plunder to members of the vendor group to be left as a loan.

Investment Agreement

While the management team's lawyer has been drawing up the acquisition agreement and negotiating this with the vendor, the venture capitalist's lawyer will not have been idle. An Investment Agreement (sometimes called a Subscription Agreement) will have been prepared to record the terms upon which the investor is to put up its money and to regulate the affairs of the company in the future. This is the key agreement from the point of view of the management team since they are parties to it and accept personal liabilities under it. The Investment Agreement lays down, (in conjunction with the Articles of Association of the Company) what the investors and management team will get out of the deal.

The Investment Agreement may contain conditions which need to be satisfied before the investor will be prepared to advance its share subscription money. In many cases these are just formalities to be dealt with. However, there are certain cases where the signing of the agreement will take place some time before completion. For instance the vendor may be required by Stock Exchange rules to get the consent of its shareholders which it will not be prepared to seek until it has signed a conditional contract with the buyout team and is secure in the knowledge that the team has conditional commitments from the financiers. In these circumstances, the conditions in the Investment Agreement become crucial from the management team's point of view since they need to be certain that they can fulfil each one or risk the company being obliged to complete the acquisition at a time when the investor is not obliged to advance the funding. Although the investor will probably insist on it, the management team should resist the imposition of conditions which are outside their control such as a condition that there shall have been no deterioration in the financial position or trading prospects of Plunder during the interval between exchange of contracts and completion.

Where there is to be a conditional contract in the true sense and an interval between exchange and completion, the question arises as to whether the warranties are simply given on exchange of contracts or whether they are deemed to have been repeated at completion. Either way, the investor will wish to have the right to back out if facts which are not to its liking come to light before completion and it is essential to ensure that the company has similar rights (called 'rights of recision') under the Acquisition Agreement.

The Investment Agreement will set out the numbers and classes of shares in the capital of the company to be subscribed for by the management team and the investor and will list the other steps to be taken simultaneously with the investment including completion of the acquisition agreement and entry by the management team into their service contracts. The relevant clause may provide for the whole of the investor's subscription money to be made available at completion or may state that there are to be staged payments which coincide with the instalments due under the Acquisition Agreement or with the prospective needs of the company for cash as it develops its business. The clause may also provide for the investor to introduce other venture capitalists after completion who will subscribe for shares on the same terms and, in the meantime, provide for the original investor to advance bridging finance.

We return now to the subject of warranties. The investment agreement will provide for warranties to be given by both the company and the individual members of the management team in favour of the investor. Although the wording of the warranty clauses here is very similar to that under the acquisition agreement the rationale of the investor in taking warranties is somewhat different to that of the vendor. The investor's primary purpose in seeking warranties is not ordinarily to obtain a right to sue the warrantors. Rather, an investor will look to the warranties as a mechanism for ensuring that there has been full and frank disclosure by the management team of the true state of affairs of the company and the management team's perception of the major risks to which the investment is subject. Having said that, no management team can afford to be reckless in giving warranties and the investor will ensure that any monetary limitations on the liabilities of the management team are sufficiently high to be of real concern to the members of the team. In addition to those relating to Plunder's business, there will be warranties as to the affairs of the company (which in a buyout situation should be totally 'clean'), the personal circumstances of the management and, in particular, their freedom to take up their new responsibilities free from any restrictions under former employment contracts.

The management team will be asked to give their warranties 'jointly and severally' which means that they will each be liable for the full amount of the investor's loss and references to knowledge of the warrantors will effectively mean the knowledge of any one of the management team. In this regard, the management team must 'sink or swim' together and trust one another to make the necessary disclosures. The worst effects of the warranties being given on a joint and several basis will be mitigated if the investor can be persuaded to agree to individual limits for the liability of each member of the team.

Having dealt with completion of the investment and given the investor the best possible assurance that it knows what it is investing in, the Investment Agreement turns its attention to the protection of the investment. The investor looks to the management team to run the business in which it has invested and so will require undertakings from each member of the team to devote his full time and attention and not to be involved in any other businesses. Where members of the team have existing outside business interests which they wish to retain this should be raised with the investor at the outset in order that the appropriate exemptions from the restrictions can be negotiated.

The investor will impose clauses which restrict the managers from becoming involved in a competing business or approaching the company's staff or customers after ceasing to be involved in the management of the company. Clearly it makes sense for these to mirror the similar restrictions under the Service Agreements. The negotiation of such restrictions should not cause undue difficulty given that the venture capitalist's lawyer will be aware that any restrictions that go beyond what is necessary to protect the legitimate interests of the investor are most unlikely to be legally enforceable.

The investor will also wish to dictate what members of the management team can and cannot do with their shareholdings. The provisions dealing with this will be split between the Investment Agreement and those parts of the Articles which deal with share transfers generally. Having backed a particular management team and insisted that the team invests personally in the venture, the investor will wish to restrict the management team from disposing of (or even raising money on security of) their shareholdings. The restrictions will last for so long as the investor holds its investment or, at the very least, a period of several years.

Conversely, the investor wishes to avoid the possibility that somebody who is no longer involved in the management of the business will continue to hold shares and benefit from the efforts of the continuing management. A member of the team who leaves the venture will be required to offer his shares for sale to the continuing members of the management team and the investor. Though the ability of the investor to force a transfer of shares by an outgoing manager has a certain logic, the provisions can operate unfairly where the manager ceases to be employed by the company through no fault of his own (for example, death or disability) or is dismissed without cause. This is particularly so when considerable past effort has been put in by the manager which has yet to be reflected in the share valuation.

The Investment Agreement will address the way in which the business of the target company is to be managed and will give to the investor veto powers by which it can prevent the company and its subsidiaries from taking certain steps without the investor's consent. The agreement will contain a long list (possibly 20 or more) of future transactions which can be blocked by the investor. Some of these are only fair in that they ensure that the business which the investor has backed is not significantly changed by the management team. For instance the investor will have approved the terms and conditions of employment of the management team and this would be rendered pointless if the team are free to re-write their service contracts the day after the investment is completed. On the other hand, some items on the list may be over-restrictive in that they would unduly interfere with the ability of the team to manage the business on a day-to-day basis. It is usually possible for the management team to negotiate some curtailment of the restrictions and an investor may be persuaded to accept that it will not withold its consent unreasonably.

The investor will also require a number of positive rights and, in particular, the right to receive regular financial and other information concerning the progress of the business. The company will have to provide regular management accounts in an agreed format and such other information as the investor may ask for. The management team will usually be required to draw up an annual budget shortly before the end of each financial year for approval by the investor. Significant departures from budget will need the investor's consent.

Notwithstanding availability of all of this information, most venture capitalists will also require the right to appoint a director to the board of the company. See Chapter Nine for a discussion of this point. The company will be required to hold board meetings regularly and to pay a fee in respect of the investor director who will attend them.

Other positive obligations which may be imposed by the investor include the maintenance by the company of adequate insurance cover (probably including key man policies taken out on the lives of the management team), compliance with legal requirements relating to the carrying on of the company's business and the right for the investor to appoint accountants to report on the affairs of the business or prepare financial information in the event that the company fails to do so.

Finally, an Investment Agreement will often look forward to the time when the investor is to realise its investment. While the investor usually recognises that it cannot oblige the management team to procure that an exit will be obtained within a given time-scale, it will usually ask the management team to acknowledge that this is the aim of the parties. The Agreement will sometimes also 'flag' that the investor will not be willing at the time of an exit to give warranties as to the affairs of the business, that it will not accept restrictions on its ability to deal with the shares it holds after a listing and that it will require any listing to enable the investor to realise a stated proportion of its shareholding. Similar points might usefully be made in relation to the management team's shareholdings.

Articles of Association

The Articles form part of the constitution of the company and regulate the activities of its shareholders and managers. The company will have had a form of Articles from the time of its incorporation, probably that laid down under companies legislation. These will be replaced by entirely new Articles which reproduce the statutory Articles and reflect the new share structure. Where the deal includes a ratchet the Articles also set out the mechanics for adjusting the percentages of share capital held by the investor and the management team.

Share Classes

You will recall that the leverage element in the transaction is introduced by the investor subscribing the bulk of its money for Preference shares. This money is in effect a loan by the investor to the company which ranks for repayment behind all other loans. Preference shares do not reflect ownership of the company but simply cash which will be repaid at some stage. It is the Ordinary, or 'equity' share capital which represents the real interest of the investor and the management team in the company's share capital. As a mechanism for enabling the investor to take special share rights and to facilitate the operation of any ratchet the investor will normally take a different class of Ordinary shares from the management team, called something like 'A' Ordinary or Preferred Ordinary shares.

The Articles will spell out the rights of the different classes of shares in relation to Dividends (reviewed in Chapter Six).

Conversion

Having saddled the company with such a complicated share structure, the investor will wish to include in the Articles the mechanics for unravelling it. This will usually involve the ability for the investor to convert its 'A' or Preferred Ordinary shares into Ordinary shares at any time, although in practice the investor would generally only do this immediately prior to an exit. The conversion provisions may also be used to achieve a ratchet adjustment (see Chapter Six).

Redemption

The preference shares will be redeemable (ie repayable) by the Company in accordance with a timetable set out in the Articles. The capital represented by the Preference shares is at risk until it is repaid and so an investor will normally give the company the option to make early redemptions. The Articles will require all of the Preference shares to be redeemed before any listing or trade sale of the company. The amount payable on redemption will usually be the price paid by the investor for the Preference shares plus all arrears and accruals of dividend.

Voting

Preference shares do not normally confer voting rights except, for example, where the company has not paid preference dividends on time. The Preferred Ordinary shares and the Ordinary shares will normally carry one vote per share and so the votes available to the investor and the management team will depend on the numbers of equity shares held. Where the investor holds a majority of the equity shares, the management team should as minority shareholders consider with their lawyer whether they need special protection under the documentation against, for instance, being removed as directors.

Class consents

The Articles will provide that the taking of certain actions by the company is a variation of the rights attaching to the investor's shares. The management team will be required to obtain the investor's consent to these variations in addition to obtaining consents as required by the investment agreement.

Share transfers

The articles will set out the limited circumstances in which shares can be transferred. For example, members of the management team may be permitted to transfer at least part of their shareholdings to their immediate family or trustees of family settlements for tax planning purposes. The investor will normally be able to transfer its shares within its corporate group, among the various funds which it manages and ultimately to the participants in those funds.

Unless a proposed transfer is specifically permitted, an outgoing shareholder will be obliged to offer his shares for sale to the other shareholders in accordance with the so called pre-emption provisions. The offer to sell must usually be at a price equivalent to the fair value of shares at the relevant time but in the early days the articles may provide for transfers by the management team to be at no more than the cost price of the shares concerned. The basic pre-emption provisions will normally provide for the shares to be offered to all shareholders pro-rata to the numbers of shares held by them, but refinements are often included whereby shares are offered first to other members of the management team so that the team collectively can continue to hold a given equity stake notwithstanding the departure of one of their number.

Where an outgoing member of the management team has been obliged to offer his shares for sale upon ceasing to be employed by the company, he may be entitled to keep a percentage of his shareholding if his departure is through no fault of his own. The investor, however, may wish to see arrangements included in the articles whereby at least a proportion of the outgoing manager's shares can be offered to a replacement manager when recruited. There is scope for much argument here but it is important to remember that when the time comes the management team as well as the investor may have decided that a particular manager 'needs to go'.

Transfer of control

Nobody will be permitted to acquire a controlling interest in the company unless he has offered to buy all of the company shares at the same price. This is to ensure that any exit will be available to shareholders generally. The proportion of the total voting rights which is regarded as giving control is ordinarily 51 per cent, but a different percentage may be appropriate depending on the sizes of the equity stakes of management and the investor.

Borrowing powers

The articles will authorise the board of directors of the company to exercise the company's borrowing powers but will limit the amounts to be borrowed. The limit specified will usually be a monetary sum, a multiple of the company's share capital and consolidated reserves or a combination of both. By having a combination, it is possible to ensure that the company has adequate powers to cover its borrowings on day one at the same time as ensuring that the amount which it may borrow will increase over time as profits are earned and retained.

Finally, with regard to the articles, it is as well for the management team and their lawyer to go through the 'standard provisions' not relating specifically to the investor's rights. Questions such as the number of directors, the quorum for board meetings, the ability to have meetings over the telephone, the use of casting votes and so on may well be of concern to the management team even if they are largely ignored by the investor and its lawyers.

Service agreements

All directors and employees of the company are legally entitled to receive from the company statements of their terms of employment dealing with such matters as responsibilities, hours of work, remuneration, pensions and grievance procedures. In the case of senior employees it is customary for this to take the form of a service contract between the individual manager and the company. The service contract will list the circumstances in which the company can sack the manager for breaches such as misconduct, absence through ill-health and so on. It will also provide for a fixed term or at least a lengthy notice period and so the manager derives comfort from the fact that, in the absence of a breach by him, he will receive monetary compensation if the agreement is terminated early or without notice. This is why investors are generally interested in keeping any fixed term or notice period to a minimum. The down-side for the executive in entering into a service contract is that it will contain restrictive covenants curtailing his ability to work for competitors for a period after ceasing to be employed by the company but, as we have seen, the manager will already have accepted restrictions of this type under the investment agreement in any case.

Loan documentation

Except where very sophisticated facilities have been negotiated, the documentation to record the loans to be made available to the company and its subsidiaries does not differ greatly from that used by banks for non-venture capital backed companies. The terms on which the facility is made available, the interest rate to be charged and the repayment provisions will be set out in a loan agreement or a facility letter and the sums advanced will be secured by the taking of standard form debentures and guarantees from the company and all companies in its new corporate group. Where there is senior debt and also a mezzanine facility, similar documentation will be used for each facility with the priority of the security taken by each lender being regulated by a separate agreement entered into by each of the lenders and the borrower.

Completion

The completion meeting should, by rights, be an ordered affair at which you will be asked to sign numerous bits of paper and hold fairly perfunctory board meetings before toasting the success of the company with champagne provided by the lawyer. In reality things are likely to be less organised because one or two of the lawyers will arrive armed with 'one or two' outstanding points to resolve. Inevitably, it seems, compromises on the most emotive points are only reached when everyone comes together for the final meeting and the stakes are sufficiently high to ensure that sense prevails on all sides.

In the absence of a genuine deadline for completion, it often makes sense to settle the documents and agree to re-convene the signing meeting once the lawyers have had time to produce fresh copies. Understandably, you will be disappointed if completion is delayed but better this than the all-night completion meeting at which mistakes are made and the lawyers' fees will start to clock up at an alarming rate. Day or night, though, bankers drafts will eventually change hands, the lawyers will move on to the next deal and the management team will return to work as owners of their business.

9

GETTING ALONG

Life after investment

Having locked his money into a small, rapidly growing company the investor faces a financial and emotional roller-coaster. He can't sell his shares when the ride gets uncomfortable—as it invariably does—and his profit will only come after years of the management conflicts, shifting markets, unforeseen setbacks, constant hunger for cash, personality clashes and frustration that make up the growth pains of a young company. Small wonder then that aftercare—the support and monitoring of an investment—is an essential part of the venture capitalist's set of skills.

As we discussed in Chapter Five, one of the most important points of differentiation between venture capital firms is the extent to which they remain involved in your business after making an investment. The phrases 'hands on' and 'hands off' are commonly used to describe investors' approaches to aftercare. The words sound self-explanatory; the hands-on approach represents a detailed, close interest in the company, while the hands-off style encompasses a passive, monitoring activity, reacting only when major events require investor input. You should regard the terms with caution when talking to investors and ensure you understand their definition, as one investor's close interest may be another's distant watching brief.

The cynical view has it that the hands-off investor makes a phone call once a year to see how things are going, while the hands-on approach is sending somebody around if the phone isn't answered to see if the company is still there.

Educating the investor

The quality of your relationship with the venture capitalist is likely to be in inverse proportion to the number of unpleasant surprises you spring, particularly soon after the investment has been completed. Sometimes these can't be helped; business is rarely a series of steady, planned achievements and you are most likely to need support of one kind or another from your investor after some piece of bad news which will probably have stretched his faith in you. Therefore you should place some emphasis during the early months after the financing on continuing the education of your investor. Build on his understanding of your markets, your business, your people and the way you operate, with two distinct objectives.

The first is to reinforce the positive elements of his decision to invest. Assessing the long-term potential of a small, high-growth company is, as you will have discovered by now, a highly subjective judgement and the venture capitalist will have made his decision to invest as a result of balancing the strengths and weaknesses of your case. Aim to convert this judgement that you have a good business into a conviction. The second objective is to deepen his understanding of the factors which influence your business.

Achieving these objectives will establish the foundation for a sound relationship with an informed and supportive investor.

Non-executive directors

As one of the investment conditions, the venture capitalist may make one or more of the following stipulations:

1.   That its own nominee is appointed a non-executive director with a specific responsibility to take care of the interests of the external investors (the 'Investor Director').

2.   That you agree to strengthen your board by the appointment of an independent non-executive director, who will have no particular brief to look after the external investor's interests but is responsible to shareholders as a whole.

3.   That you agree to appoint a non-executive chairman, again responsible to shareholders as a whole.

The investor director

When will an investor director be appointed? Almost invariably, the investor will insist on the right to appoint a non-executive director, although he may inform you that he does not intend to exercise it unless things go seriously awry.

You can expect the investor to appoint a director at the time of the investment:

- when the investment is large, either in absolute terms (any company with over £1 million or so in venture capital money will usually have an investor director) or relative to the investor's portfolio;

● when it is particularly high risk;

● when the investor is able to appoint an individual who can make a specific contribution to the company.

These latter two points are often embraced in early stage investments, where the investor wants to keep a particularly close eye on progress and at the same time is able to strengthen the management team in a specific area, usually marketing or finance.

Who will it be? Practice varies. The investor may appoint one of its own executives or may nominate an external individual to take care of its interests. Often the investor has to resolve the conflict between appointing one of its own employees or an independent consultant. The advantage with appointing its own employee is that he will have the investor's interests in mind and, as he will normally be the executive who negotiated the transaction, will already have a good relationship with the management team. On the other hand an independent consultant is more likely to be able to offer specific expertise and contacts, but not being an employee of the investor is in danger of 'going native' and losing sight of the investor's interests.

In any event, the investor is unlikely to insist on the appointment of an individual with whom you do not feel you can work (although he will retain the right ultimately to appoint whomever he pleases).

What does he do? The primary role of the investor director is to monitor your progress, which he will do through the media of board meetings and monthly management reports (see below). However he is also highly motivated to make positive contributions. The area which entrepreneurs find most useful is the addition of an objective voice to the board discussions.

Even if he has no relevant specialised expertise, you can draw on his generic knowledge of the problems which face small companies. He may be able to contribute in the following areas:

1. Strategic planning and policy. A non executive director with general management experience is often able to fill a gap in the management team's own set of skills, particularly if they are building a business for the first time. Building the foundation for a larger company, with its attendant management structure, financial and logistic implications may be outside the team's experience, yet is

a generic business discipline in which a non-executive with experience of growth can contribute.

2.   Acquisitions. The venture capitalist, with a broader view of the business community, a wide range of contacts and specific experience of valuing and acquiring businesses, can often play a leading role in targeting and making acquisitions.

3.   Personnel traumas. The non-executive director is often able to build bridges when personality clashes or fundamental disagreements split the management team. He can play the honest broker role, as all parties can appreciate that his sole interest is the future of the company.

4.   Financial planning. The venture capitalist will have experience of the major financings which happen only a few times in a company's lifetime and which are likely to be unfamiliar to the executive directors.

For the smaller, younger companies the investor is more likely to appoint an individual with a more specific contribution to make, in areas such as technology development and marketing. Again the emphasis of his contribution will be in the provision of a broad, objective view but it will be within the context of his knowledge of your particular industry or market.

Board meetings

Nothing is guaranteed to destroy your relationship with your investors more quickly than holding meetings which, although called board meetings, are in fact no more than carefully staged monthly presentations to the investor director. Use board meetings for their proper purpose, which is to discuss and make decisions on the strategic and major operational issues facing the company. Draw the investor director into active participation and do not attempt to hide or disguise disagreements or arguments in your team.

Information flow

You should aim to provide the investor, every month, with Management Accounts—Profit and Loss Account, Balance Sheet and Cashflow, for the month and year to date, with comparisons with budget. You should also provide a Managing Director's Report—a narrative summary of progress during the month and major issues facing the company.

'You are relying on the (venture capitalist's) advice for the nuts and bolts of the management team . . . you pay them a hell of a lot of money to come and sit on your wretched board; they've got to contribute. And they can . . . they will provide a bouncing board and they will also provide a Spanish Inquisition. Both are very useful.

It is an excellent discipline once a month to make yourself sit down . . . and write out a progress report. Because under each heading you have got to think 'have I done what I said I was going to do and does that make sense—what sort of questions will be asked?

I think one of the things you've got to be quite careful of is . . . making certain that you keep a board structure which is conducive to doing what boards should do which is make proper decisions rather than . . . giving every current or potential investor a say in what is going on.'

James Heneage

'I feel more comfortable in a company our size, when we have names like (the investors) with us because first of all they improve our credibility within the financial sector, even if within our industry they don't, but also they have expertise and experience beyond that of myself and the rest of my shareholders and directors and I think it is very important that we listen to them.'

Paul Smith

Annual budgets

The investor will generally have the right to approve or veto the adoption of a new budget. This raises the potential for conflict, as the budget itself is built upon detailed assumptions and information fully known and understood only by the executive management team, so the investor director is in a weak position from which to either analyse it in depth or suggest changes. Generally, however, the investor will seek to be satisfied that the budget is realistic, reflects a continuation of the business strategy on which he invested (or a revised strategy subsequently agreed with him), and shows further progress towards his objective of earning a return on his investment.

The process of preparing a new annual budget provides an excellent opportunity to review with the investor your progress, changes in external conditions and the company's prospects. Once you have a draft budget, it is worth while to arrange a special meeting with the investor director, outside the normal board meetings, to review it and talk through the assumptions behind it and your expectations for the coming year. A discussion such as this, which looks slightly beyond the day-to-day issues which dominate board meetings, can be extremely effective in shaping the investor's perception of how well you are doing.

Some investors request that a new three- or five-year business plan is prepared every year, in order to ensure that your long-term strategic thinking is regularly revised and updated.

Further rounds

Venture capital firms earmark a portion—typically between 20 and 40 per cent—of their funds for further rounds of equity finance for companies in their portfolio. They rarely know which investments will need further support, only that some will.

Further rounds can be divided into two categories—welcome and unwelcome. This should need no further elaboration; investors welcome the opportunity to back success by providing further funds for companies to fund acquisition or genuine expansion, while you will get a less positive reception when asking for further support because you have failed to meet the business plan and have run out of cash.

However things are rarely so clear in practice, especially from the entrepreneur's point of view. Typically, having failed to meet the first year or two's forecasts, his gaze will have shifted to a bigger opportunity which is three or five years away and it is to pursue this that further funds will be needed. The original business plan is declared redundant. This is not an approach guaranteed to win investors' hearts or confidence. It is true that many ultimately viable businesses require more time and capital to achieve profitability than was originally envisaged (Federal Express in the USA is one of the most famous—or notorious—examples, requiring no less than five rounds of funding before becoming profitable.) However the decision for the investor is a tough one, asked as he is to increase his exposure to a team which has failed to achieve its objectives.

It is at this time that the work you have devoted to building a relationship with the investor will pay off. The more he understands about your business, your management and your markets the more likely he is to be supportive—or at least to make a decision for the right reasons.

Terms of further rounds

You will hear the phrase 'wipe out' terms applied used in the context of further rounds. It refers to a situation where the new money takes such a large proportion of the company's equity that existing investors and management are diluted to very small stakes. When this happens, it generally does so not because the investors are taking advantage of the Company's weak position but as a result of the application of the kind of arithmetic we discussed in Chapter Six. If all of the first round investor's money has been spent, and a profitable exit is as far away now as it was when the first investment was made, then the existing equity holders can expect to be diluted down to the kind of level which the management alone held previously.

The investors, whether they are your existing backers providing further funds or new players, will of course need to balance the requirements of their investment arithmetic with the need to make sure that management is left with a sufficiently large stake of the equity to ensure their continued commitment. Also, existing investors are unlikely to agree to terms which dilute their holdings unreasonably, although any investor who is not providing further support in a crisis refinancing has little negotiating strength.

Exits

The end of the line for the investor is probably—provided that the exit is not involuntary by way of a receivership or liquidation—just another phase in the company's growth so far as you are concerned. As we mentioned in Chapter One, there are four ways in which an investor can realise his investment in your company; an acquisition by another company, a public flotation, a sale to another investor or a sale to the company's management (or, as permitted by the Companies Act 1981, a sale of his shares to the company itself).

Each of these activities is a specialist area which deserves a book to itself. The intricacies of valuing and selling private companies or achieving stock market flotations are beyond the scope of this guide and are presumably of little direct interest to you at this stage of raising finance.

The only point that needs to be made is a reminder that, when you accepted the investor's cheque, you accepted a moral, although not a legal, obligation to do your best to enable him to realise his investment. One of the most frustrating experiences for a venture capitalist is to be invested in a management team who run out of ambition or ideas before growing their company to sufficient size or profitability to enable an investor to sell his shareholding. These companies are referred to as the 'living dead' by the industry, a macabre phrase which sums up their contribution. Don't sit back on an unquoted investor's money with mediocre performance, a comfortable life-style and no ambition.

The essence of venture capital is the partnership between entrepreneur and finance. Although the terms of this partnership can be reduced to arithmetic and legal documentation, the qualities which make it successful are the relationship between the two sides and the mutual understanding of different, but complementary goals.

10

CORPORATE PARTNERS

Corporate venturing

by
Kathryn Dunn of NEDO Corporate Venturing Centre

What is corporate venturing?

Corporate venturing is a term used to describe partnerships between large, established companies and innovative, young companies.

It is neither a licensing agreement nor an acquisition but involves creating a partnership which shares resources, shares risks and shares benefits.

Implicit in seeking venture capital from any source is the plan for growth. In looking directly at the issue of growth and means of achieving it, it is not always necessary to think in terms of growing all the resources needed organically, funded by increased shareholders' funds. An alliance with a well-established company, which has a direct interest in the growth of your business can bring a portfolio of resources into play much more quickly. These may include market information, access to international sales force, technical support, management advice and enhanced credibility with suppliers and customers.

To justify such a partnership you will have to have something to offer the larger company which is of commercial significance to it. This could include product innovation which fits with its marketing strategy, a highly skilled and creative team which it would be hard to retain in-house or a technical service which extends its knowledge of the market-place. There is often an emphasis on technology; however the important point is not so much the technology, but an element of commercial value which it is difficult for the larger company to generate itself.

What shape might an alliance take?

At one end of the spectrum are licensing deals and marketing agreements in which you transfer the rights to exploit a product or technology in a defined market area to another company in exchange for royalties on sales and/or lump sum payments. However this is basically a disposal of one section of your business and here we are really concerned with some form of ongoing collaboration. This can involve setting up a joint venture with a larger company or bringing the larger company directly into your business as either a minority or a majority shareholder.

Your aim is both to raise the necessary development funding and to have a commitment from the larger company to support the growth of your business. To implement this commitment you will need an additional agreement with the corporate partner to cover the operational areas of collaboration.

Formulating and agreeing a partnership with a corporate can be more difficult than with a venture capital investor for a number of reasons:

1. The aims and needs of the large corporate are more complex than those of an investment fund. Although both require realisable capital gain, the corporate will be looking for additional benefits and the choice of the particular corporate as a partner may have a greater impact on the development of the business than the choice of venture capital fund.

2. The corporate will need commitment to the partnership both at head office level and at divisional/operational level. You will need to establish a good working relationship with both parties.

3. The corporate may be less familiar than a venture capitalist with an entrepreneurial culture and with forming partnerships. To cope with this the corporate may either prefer a venture capital fund to invest alongside, or it may have subcontracted the management of its own venture capital fund to specialist investment fund managers. One of your tasks in dealing with a potential corporate partner will be to identify its own decision-making process on the partnership.

4. The corporate may not be working to a particular deadline on evaluating and establishing a partnership. This will be less of a problem when you have a technology, product or service which meets a critical need which the corporate has already identified and/or you have alternative discussions in hand.

On the other hand if there is a strong rationale for the partnership, and the large corporate already has a positive policy on corporate venturing at board level, then it can often move faster than a venture capital fund in proposing a structure for a partnership. This is because its interests are more focused and it has practical, operational knowledge of the relevant industry structure, market and technology.

Why do large corporates undertake corporate venturing?

In assessing whether a corporate partner is right for your business, you
will need to understand why it is interested in this form of co-operation.
Traditionally joint ventures have been used for tackling markets and
production in foreign countries where a partnership with locals facili-
tates adaptation to the local culture. Today companies are using partnership with smaller, innovative companies to cope with increasingly
rapid changes in technology, legislation, demarcation between markets
and industries, and geographical and economic boundaries.

The corporate venture is a vehicle for coping with uncertainty, rapid
change and experimentation. Hence certain areas of industry have seen
a higher level of corporate venturing activity. These include:

- The computer industry which, focusing on data collection and
  analysis, has blurred into telecommunications with long dis-
  tance exchange of information;

- Pharmaceuticals, chemicals and agricultural industries which are
  adapting to and incorporating biotechnology;

- Companies seeking a window on the single European market
  without full commitment of acquisition;

- Newly privatised companies wishing to maximise the use of their
  inherited, protected market and to foster commercial management.

Two examples of European companies with active corporate venturing
activities are Olivetti and British Gas. The former has for many years
been partnering companies in IT and telecommunications throughout
Europe and occasionally the USA. British Gas has recently set up a fund

to invest in businesses which benefit the exploration for, and production of, gas and oil; gas transmission and distribution; or which support and develop the applications and use of gas.

From the small company side a British start-up with sensor technology formed a partnership with Baxter Healthcare which enabled their products for blood glucose manufacturing for diabetics to become a leading product both in the American and European markets.

One of the reasons frequently put forward by major companies for embarking on corporate venturing is the search for entrepreneurial management. There is a recognition that this can be hard to develop and maintain in-house but new business development can be dependent on it. Apart from the vision of a market opportunity and how to exploit it, the entreprenuer is valued for having the judgement and knowledge to make and implement critical decisions quickly, to be able to operate with a lean overhead and to be resourceful. Other skills required are to keep a small team committed and driving forward, to manage cashflow and to manage growth.

In identifying a potential partner's strategic needs for participating in a venture with yourselves, you also need to consider its organisational structure and management style. Some large corporates consist of a multiplicity of small businesses with more or less overlapping manufacturing skills and R & D needs; some have a long tradition of innovation; others will have been focusing on stabilisation in declining or mature industries and now be looking to establish a basis for renewed growth.

There are two fundamental organisational issues which the corporate will have had to address internally before embarking on a partnership. The first is participation in businesses where it does not have ultimate control. The second is working with entrepreneurs who have salaries, benefits and prospects of capital gain which may be potentially much greater than the corporate's own internal staff (albeit that you, the entrepreneur, have taken greater personal risk to be in that position).

Fairly decentralised companies where divisional directors maintain a good access to head office strategic decision-makers can often handle corporate venturing most comfortably.

Structuring the partnership

There are no hard and fast rules for structuring a corporate venture but there are lessons to be learnt from other people's experience. They can be summarised in three basic principles:

1.   Both parties must specify and agree the aims of the partnership.

2. The resources to be contributed by each party must be identified.

3. Assume the partnership is temporary and agree a procedure for parting.

It is useful to think of the partnership as both an investment agreement with the corporate and an operational agreement. The disciplines for assessing the level of investment and the share structure are the same as for investment from a venture capital fund. Major companies do, however, vary considerably in their policy on shareholding levels. Some will prefer to keep the equity stake to less than 20 per cent. At this level in the UK, they do not need to consolidate your results in their own annual accounts.

You should also give consideration as to whether your corporate partner should be represented on your board. Often with a venture capital fund investor, any director it may put on the board of an investee company is able to contribute experience of management of other small companies aiming at high growth. In the case of a corporate partner it is less likely that they will be able to contribute this particular expertise although there are exceptions to this. A director on your board may, however, prove a useful champion of the business within the corporate.

In arriving at an agreement it is necessary not just to convince the corporate that your business is worth investing in but also to gain their commitment and co-operation to making it work. To do this it is useful to develop a business strategy and plan of implementation together with the corporate. In doing this you will not only clarify the objectives of both parties, but identify the resources each is to put into the business, as well as lay the ground for the personal working relationships necessary to make the partnership effective. Good personal chemistry between the individuals involved is critical.

By working on a joint plan, you will be able to justify the level and time-scale of funding required. You will also need to agree:

- a framework for review and revision of strategy and plan;

- procedure for arranging additional funding
  —does the corporate partner have first option?
  —should there be restrictions on additional corporate partners?

- method for ending the partnership
  —do you and the partner have the first option of buying out each other's shareholding?
  —how will you establish a market price?

You will also need to develop a procedure for handling disagreements and to be clear as to areas of discretion in decision-making.

It may be tempting for the corporate to want you to follow its normal financial and management accounting and reporting structures. The advice from both large and small companies with experience of corporate venturing is that this should be avoided.

Your company will have significantly different needs both in timing and nature of management information. The administrative overhead that can be implicit in corporate reporting could be disastrous. More important is that you agree with your partner what are the critical events about which they need to be kept informed.

On the operational side you may need agreements covering marketing, exchange of and use of technology and contribution to further R & D.

For example, if the aim of the partnership is that the corporate takes on international marketing of some or all of your products, you will need an agreement which specifies:

- which markets it will address;

- on which products it will have first right of refusal;

- under what circumstances the marketing rights will revert to you.

You will also need agreements on exchange of relevant technical information. In terms of protection of know-how and marketing rights all the normal disciplines of licensing apply. The main point here is to decide where the profit-taking will be. For example a product might be transferred to the corporate at cost price but a royalty paid on the sales made by the partner. You must also decide what constraints there should be on information flow between the partners.

The latter may apply to the basic technology of the product, the manufacturing process, market information and management accounts. It is a question of balancing the need to maintain the value within the partnership and the information required by the partner to evaluate investing and to monitor that investment, together with the cross-flow of information required for effective co-operation.

If you are looking for technical support in production engineering or defence of patents then there will need to be restriction on the use to which the corporate partner can put this information. Alternatively, if the partner only needs access to your final product and is providing market feedback to help specify the second and third generation products which you are developing then the partner need not have access to your premises.

You may also want to keep strict control over which of your personnel can deal with your partner.

Managing the partnership

Be pro-active in managing the partnership. Problems are bound to arise but by anticipating them you can also prepare for some of the solutions.

The most common source of conflict is non-performance of your business. While the reasons for non-performance can be many and varied, the conflict can be reduced if the partner was involved in preparing the business plan for the partnership, and you have kept the corporate informed of problems encountered and slippage, together with the action you are taking to deal with it.

The joint business plan should cover all that a normal business plan would cover (see Chapter Four). It enables a joint commitment to the strategy and financial performance. In addition the partners should agree rules of operation and areas of discretion.

You should not regard your partner as a soft touch for extra money. No investor, corporate or otherwise, wants to put good money after bad. However, if you have maintained the confidence of the partner in your management and the long-term viability and growth of business, its continued support will be easier to agree. At the same time if the partnership's problems start to take up an inordinate amount of the corporate's management time they may prefer to cut their losses and end the partnership.

However, even if your business is performing well, there can be problems. For instance:

- you develop a product, not anticipated at time of partnership, which competes directly with your partner;

- a change of ownership of your corporate partner;

- your partner invests in a competitor;

- the 'corporate venturing champion' within your partner leaves.

All these could threaten the effectiveness of the partnership. These risks can be mitigated if you have:

- ensured that you develop good personal working relationships with both head office and operational staff in the corporate and not become over-dependent on one individual as a point of contact;

- agreed limits on areas of influence and access to information;

- agreed a framework for raising further funding both from the corporate partner and other sources;

- agreed a procedure for parting company at the election of either party.

Rules of thumb

The success or otherwise of a corporate partnership is ultimately assessed by all parties in terms of capital gain.

Understand the culture of your corporate partner and how your company is viewed within it. Is this a one-off partnership for them, in exceptional circumstances? Or are you part of a structured strategy for corporate venturing with many innovative firms? Understand what are the critical aspects of your business which should not be divulged to your partner and police this.

Understand what your alternative strategies are. Ensure that your expectations of the partnership are agreed with the partners.

Avoid being pulled into the corporate bureaucracy. Part of your advantage is quick decision-making and flexibility. Keep it.

APPENDIX I

Haigh Castle & Co
A Case Study

A management buyin engineered within six days

by

Stephen Welton and David Williamson

There is a perception that the timescale for a management buyin transaction is rather longer than for a sale to a trade bidder. The buyin of Haigh Castle belies this perception. Contracts were exchanged within six days, yet the due diligence was as thorough as necessary. Getting to exchange of contracts in such a short period is not easy, but it is, on occasions, necessary and there can be real benefits to speed in transactions such as this. Management attention can be distracted from the running of the business during negotiations and this is in no-one's interests. This case history shows that it can be achieved by a happy co-operation and co-ordination among all the members of the team.

Haigh Castle & Co

Haigh Castle & Co was formed in 1956 as a company specialising in the importation of canned foods as an agent for overseas suppliers. It subsequently expanded its business to include buying canned goods as principal for onward sale to the UK grocery trade. In the early 1960s the business was sold to S & W Berisford. Under Berisford, the importing and distribution business was separated from the agency business, and merged with Berisford's other food importing interests to form Berisford Foods. The agency business continued within the Berisford Group as Haigh Castle.

Berisfood Foods inherited Berisford's and Haigh Castle's long standing contracts and developed them to good effect. In addition to marketing its own brands, Berisford Foods so successfully developed its customers' private label division that it became one of the primary suppliers of private label salmon and corned beef to the UK grocery trade, a position currently maintained by Haigh Castle.

In January 1987, Hunter Saphir acquired a number of businesses from Berisford, including Berisford Foods (subsequently renamed HS Foods) and Haigh Castle. Two years later, Hunter Saphir decided to dispose of these two businesses in order to concentrate on its core business, which is chilled food distribution.

The activities of the businesses for sale fell under four different headings:

- **Branded traditional canned foods.** These comprise a range of canned fish, meats, fruits and vegetables. They are sourced from overseas suppliers and marketed under the Osprey and Cucumber (fish), Ship (meats and tomatoes) and Orchard Price (fruit and vegetables) labels.

- **Private label traditional canned goods.** A variety of canned foods are imported and sold to private label customers, principally major multiples.

- **Other products**. Drinking chocolate granules, imported from Germany, are sold to private label customers. Management plans to sell the product under the German distributor's name have since been implemented. The range also includes pasta, step can and fruit in jars.

- **Private label agency business**. The company acts as agent, sourcing products for private label sale. The principal products are corned beef and salmon. A full service is provided, including procurement, shipping, storing and delivering the goods, for which the company is paid a commission.

Salmon and corned beef are by far the dominant elements of the product mix. Sales in the financial year to February 1988 amounted to £45.4 million, with Haigh Castle claiming about ten per cent of the UK canned fish market and eight per cent of the UK canned meats market. The canned fruit and vegetable share of the market was smaller.

J Sainsbury, Marks & Spencer and Tesco are the three largest customers. The remainder of the company's sales are broadly spread throughout the entire food retailing sector, including all the major multiples.

The salmon is sourced principally from Canada and the Soviet Union and there are long standing relationships with suppliers in both countries. There are similarly well established contacts in Brazil, source of the majority of the corned beef.

The storage and distribution of the product is subcontracted. Quality control is the responsibility of the company. Suppliers are visited regularly and samples of the imported goods are analysed continuously by technical and commercial staff on arrival in the UK.

It will be seen that effective relationship management was the key to success in Haigh Castle's market. The company had no manufacturing or processing input to the product range. Its role was to secure supplies of quality products at competitive prices and to distribute these reliably to its customer base.

Pricing of the product was important, but no more so than the reliability of supplies and quality control. Haigh Castle had established an excellent reputation in these areas during its 30 years of existence.

As with any distribution business, working capital management is crucial with so much of the value of the operation tied up in stocks and debtors as the balance sheet below indicates.

Summary balance sheet at 29 February 1988 (£000s)

Fixed assets		54
Current assets		
Cash	0	
Debtors	4,360	
Stocks	5,245	
Prepayments	167	
Total current assets		9,772
Current liabilities		
Creditors	1,687	
Accruals	47	
Tax payable	97	
Total current liabilities		1,831
Net current assets		7,941
Total assets less current liabilities		7,995
Long term liabilities		5,472
Net assets		2,523

Ordinary share capital	109
Retained earnings	2,414

Ordinary shareholders' funds	2,523

In January 1989, Granville was engaged to conduct an acquisition search for David Shelton. As part of the preliminary due diligence, references were taken up on David Shelton, and one referee nominated was John Saphir of Hunter Saphir. Saphir thus became aware that David Shelton was seeking an opportunity and suggested HS Foods and Haigh Castle.

Granville and Security Pacific EuroFinance began preliminary analysis of the transaction, but it was clear that Hunter Saphir's attentions were directed more keenly at a third party and preliminary analysis was very limited. However, when a delay occurred with the third party negotiations, the buyin team used this as an opportunity to enter with a new offer.

On Wednesday 22 February, Hunter Saphir indicated that the other bidder (being a listed company) required shareholder approval (which would extend the estimated completion date by one month and create a conditional contract). Hunter Saphir would be willing to accept the buyin offer if contracts could be exchanged six days later to allow the usage of paperwork, circulars etc. that would have to be expensively reworked post-28 February, their financial year-end. If not, the sale may be completed with the third party after Hunter Saphir's year-end.

In order to appreciate what was achieved in the six days up to 28 February it is necessary to understand how things stood at 22 February.

In the preliminary discussions David Shelton had met Bruce Daly and Martin Parry, two key members of the incumbent management team. They had been able to reach an informal agreement to work together as a team if this transaction could be arranged. Thus the transaction would be a combined management buyin/buyout which is not uncommon in these situations.

The management team

It was regarded as important to retain existing management, particularly since the business was dependent upon the long standing relationship with customers and suppliers.

The makeup of the management team would enable continuity in running the existing business while profiting from the leadership and expertise of a new managing director brought in from outside.

David Shelton had had considerable success in building up the chilled foods division at Norpak. He had been chief executive of an autonomous subsidiary of Christian Salvesen. His other experience included periods as a food analyst at Vickers Da Costa, now known as Scrimgeour Vickers, and operations director at Levi-Strauss.

Bruce Daly had been a director of all the companies in the target group since 1969. He is well regarded as an expert in the salmon industry and is well respected throughout the trade as a senior figure.

Martin Parry had been appointed finance director of Haigh Castle five years earlier, having previously been finance director and company secretary of another Berisford subsidiary.

Granville had been appointed by Shelton to conduct a formal acquisition search and, in the course of the preliminary discussions with Hunter Saphir, had approached Security Pacific EuroFinance to provide senior debt and mezzanine finance for the venture.

On the vendor's side, Hunter Saphir had already gone a long way towards securing a deal with a third party, so much of the information and documentation was already in place. Nevertheless, as the following reveals, there was a considerable amount of work to be done by the team in order to exchange contracts within six days.

Haigh Castle was a profitable business at the time of the transaction. Operating profit on the turnover of £45.4 million was £1.6 million. Nevertheless, there were opportunities for improving efficiency.

The management plans to improve profitability had three elements: revenue growth, distribution cost control and tighter management of working capital.

Revenue growth

Revenue growth of nine per cent per annum was projected for the next three years. This would come from three areas: new product lines sold to multiples; greater exploitation of growth markets; and a move with existing products into new markets.

Distribution cost control

Haigh Castle had been the first contract of any real size for the distributor. The service had been good, but there was a feeling that the contract was ripe for renegotiation, with consequent cost reduction.

Working capital control

There is no better way to understand a business than to see how cash is turned back into cash. Haigh Castle is a good example of this. The business was all about procurement, warehousing and distribution. Efficiencies in working capital control would have a pronounced effect on the company's financial health.

At the time of the buyout, the company had inventories equivalent to 50 days sales. Management believed that this could be cut down to 30 days without reducing the quality of service. The service point is vital. Relationship management was a key element in the success of the business and this might appear to be in conflict with the objectives of reducing inventory levels. Quality of services can be maintained, however, by a more careful matching of purchases with projected orders. This would be a consequence of a new computerised inventory control system.

When it came to constructing the financial package for the transaction, it was recognised that the potential for inventory level reduction was strong but, to be prudent, a reduction to 45 days rather than 30 was assumed.

The other key elements in working capital management are the control of receivables and payables. The management aimed to improve the accounts receivable turn by two days and the accounts payable turn by up to ten days. Again, this seemed to be a possibility.

Nevertheless, the company was dealing with both customers and suppliers who had no misunderstanding of the importance of their own working capital management. It was therefore important that the transaction was not structured to be totally dependent on these improvements being achieved.

The structure of the deal

The consideration for the acquisition was agreed at net asset value plus £450,000. This gave an anticipated consideration of £9.1 million plus expenses estimated at £0.5 million less cash in the business of £0.25 million—a total financial requirement of £9.35 million. In addition, Haigh Castle required various banking facilities totalling £1.25 million for guarantees to Customs and Excise and documentary credits.

As usual with transactions of this sort, the management had a ratchet arrangement as an incentive to performance. The 'A' ordinary shares are to be converted to ordinary shares or partly redeemed in 1992, depending on the aggregate level of pre-tax profits achieved in the three years ending 29 February 1992.

The capital structure

		£000s
Granville	'A' ordinary shares	650
	Preference shares	1,350
Management	'A' ordinary shares	100
		2,100
Security Pacific		
EuroFinance	Evergreen revolving loan facility	5,750
	Mezzanine facility	1,500
	Guarantee facility	1,250
	Total	**£10,600**

The effect of this ratchet arrangement on the management's shareholdings is illustrated below:

Aggregate profits (£000s)	Management shareholding
5,000 or above	25.1%
4,000	18.0%
3,000 or below	10.9%

No ordinary share dividends are projected to be paid before 1992.

Management were able to raise their investment on short notice from personal resources.

The preference shares carry a net fixed dividend of 10.5 per cent (14 per cent gross) pa, payable on 1 March and September, commencing 1 September 1989. The net dividend increases to 12 per cent with effect from 1 March 1992 and the preference shares are redeemable in three equal instalments in 1992, 1993, and 1994, or earlier on sale, flotation or at the company's option.

The summary balance sheet shows that the loan would need to be secured on the current assets. This kind of security sometimes causes concern at lending institutions, although there is no real reason why this should be so. An analysis of the quality of these assets is necessary.

At Haigh Castle, Security Pacific EuroFinance found a very high quality of accounts receivable. Ninety-eight per cent were paid within 60 days of invoice and there was a low bad debt history. There was some concern at the level of concentration—the ten largest accounts accounted for 80 per cent of receivable value—but these were all large well-rated multiples with whom Haigh Castle had enjoyed a long and secure relationship. Accordingly, Security Pacific EuroFinance was comfortable to advance 85 per cent of accounts receivable up to 90 days from invoice date.

Inventory was considered a suitable security. The canned products have a long shelf life, so long as they are not stored in damp conditions where rust can become a problem. As such, the bank was able to advance 60 per cent of inventory levels with the total advance capped at £4 million.

The receivable and inventory in total did not provide sufficient collateral on day one. The borrowing base projected a shortfall of £0.5 million initially. Management's projections showed the shortfall increasing to £1.5 million in the first nine months of the buyout. After one year, it was projected that the collateral shortfall would be cured through trading profits and no longer required.

Security Pacific EuroFinance provided an evergreen revolving credit facility of £7.25 million of which £1.5 million was a mezzanine facility and £1.25 million a banking facility for guarantees and documentary credits.

The evergreen revolving credit facility is structured to expand as the working capital needs of the business grow.

The interest rate is LIBOR + 1.75 per cent to LIBOR + three per cent depending on the level of outstanding debt.

At the time of writing, six months have elapsed since the transaction. All the indications are that the company is on target to trigger the maximum stake for the management. The plans they had conceived are being put into practice with encouraging revenue and income growth. The computerised inventory control system is being phased in and positive results are already apparent. The buyin was well received by the workforce which might have faced redundancy if the alternative sale to a competitor had taken place.

The facilities provided by Security Pacific EuroFinance have been increased further to £10.5 million (£9 million for the evergreen revolving credit facility and £1.5 million banking facility).

Haigh Castle is now seeking to broaden its interests in the food industry. Its unique relationships with suppliers and customers can be used for a wider range of services. Haigh Castle expects to embark on an acquisition programme before long. It is already engaged in an active search programme.

There are a few general lessons which can be learned from this deal. It was the very process of Granville undertaking a formal acquisition search for David Shelton which led to the possibility at Hunter Saphir.

We believe that Granville and Security Pacific EuroFinance made a formidable team in financing the transaction to effectively outbid a trade buyer. We had known each other for some time and this gave the relationship a basis of mutual understanding and trust. There was a need for swiftness and flexibility in arranging the deal to which both sides were able to contribute.

Furthermore, Haigh Castle has strong financial controls and records in place so that the reviews and investigations required were able to be completed very thoroughly in a short time-frame. This significantly enhanced the speed at which the transaction was completed. Also, to have the support and participation of the resident management contributed to the success of the transaction.

Stephen Welton is a vice president and head of acquisition finance for Security Pacific EuroFinance. David Williamson is a corporate finance director with Granville & Co. London.

Diary of the deal

Wednesday 22 February 1989

Morning	It appeared that the MBI of Haigh Castle was unlikely to occur because of an earlier offer from another buyer.
6.00 pm	Telephone call from Hunter Saphir indicates delays and problems with buyer. Hunter Saphir now says it will sell to the buyin team if completion can be by its year end, namely the following Tuesday, 28 February.
6.30 pm–8.00 pm	Security Pacific EuroFinance and Granville meet to discuss the transaction again and decide to increase the price by £500,000 and to attempt to complete within the time frame.

Thursday 23 February 1989

8.00 am– 9.30 am   Security Pacific EuroFinance and Granville hold internal meetings to allocate responsibilities.

Afternoon   Granville meeting with Hunter Saphir to discuss initial terms.

Afternoon   Meeting between Granville and law firm Gouldens to give instructions and make initial decisions on documentation.

Evening   Meeting between Granville and Security Pacific EuroFinance to set up arrangements for visiting the company in order to make detailed review of operations.

Evening   Meeting between Granville and Security Pacific EuroFinance to hammer out the proposed loan structure of the deal.

Friday 24 February 1989

Well before sunrise   Security Pacific EuroFinance staff drive to Middlewich to start review of the company. Waiting for permission to enter company at 10.00 am.

Morning   Letter of Offer sent to Hunter Saphir and access granted to Security Pacific EuroFinance to review the records of Haigh Castle.

Afternoon   Security Pacific EuroFinance instruct law firm Wilde Sapte which starts reviewing the Acquisition Agreement and drafting the loan documentation.

Afternoon   Granville sends final copy of Investment Memorandum to Investment Committees.

Saturday 25 February 1989

Afternoon   Security Pacific EuroFinance finishes work at the company and returns to London to analyse results.

All day   All lawyers continue the drafting of the documentation.

Sunday 26 February 1989

All day   Security Pacific EuroFinance analyses information and starts to put loan memorandum together.

All day   Lawyers continue to work on the documentation.

Monday 27 February 1989

Morning   Granville's London Investment Committee approves deal.

Morning   Security Pacific EuroFinance distribute loan request and mezzanine investment memorandum to credit committee.

Morning   Security Pacific EuroFinance meets with Wilde Sapte to review drafts of loan documentation.

Afternoon   Security Pacific EuroFinance receives local approval.

Afternoon to early morning   Granville, Security Pacific EuroFinance, Gouldens and Wilde Sapte complete negotiations on the Sale and Purchase Agreement with Hunter Saphir and their lawyers as well as finalising the loan documentation.

Tuesday 28 February 1989

Morning   Final commercial details agreed with Hunter Saphir.

Morning   Board of Granville's Jersey Funds approves investment.

All day   All lawyers continue to negotiate on legal details.

Evening   Security Pacific EuroFinance receives credit approval from California

Before Midnight   Exchange of contracts

The purchaser was in fact a Granville shelf company Laxgate, which subsequently entered into agreements with the management team.

Appendix II

The following list of companies represents the full membership of the British Venture Capital Association. For *full* details of these companies and their investment activities, please contact the BVCA Secretariat at:

3 Catherine Place
London SW1E 6DX
Tel: 071-233 5212
Fax: 071-931 0563

ABACUS DEVELOPMENT CAPITAL LIMITED
4 Queen Anne Mews,
London W1M 9DF
Telephone: 071-323 5224
Fax: 071-631 3486

Minimum Investment: £100,000
Stage of Investment: All stages supported
Contact: Wendy Pollecoff

ABERDEEN FUND MANAGERS LTD
10 Queen's Terrace,
Aberdeen AB9 1QJ
Telephone: 0224 631999
Fax: 0224 647010

Minimum Investment: Abtrust—£100,000
    Radiotrust—£50,000
Stage of Investment: Development, MBO etc
Contact: Hugh WM Little

ABINGWORTH MANAGEMENT LTD
26 St. James's Street,
London SW1A 1HA
Telephone: 071-839 6745
Fax: 071-930 1891

Minimum Investment: £250,000
Stage of Investment: All stages
Contact: Anthony Montagu

ADVENT LIMITED
25 Buckingham Gate,
London SW1E 6LD
Telephone: 071-630 9811
Fax: 071-828 1474/071-828 4919

Minimum Investment: £250,000
Stage of Investment: All stages, but not
    highly leveraged deals
Contact: Colin Amies

ADVENT INTERNATIONAL PLC
39 Victoria Street,
London SW1H 0ED
Telephone: 071-333 0800
Fax: 071-333 0801

Minimum Investment: £500,000
Stage of Investment: Expansion, MBO, MBI,
    LBO
Contact: Douglas R Brown

ADVENT MANAGEMENT OPPORTUNITIES LIMITED
25 Buckingham Gate,
London SW1E 6LD
Telephone: 071-828 6944
Fax: 071-828 9958

Minimum Investment: £500,000
Stage of Investment: Expansion and management buy-in
Contact: John Nash

AIB VENTURE CAPITAL
12 Old Jewry,
London EC2R 8DP
Telephone: 071-606 5800
Fax: 071-606 5818

Minimum Investment: £200,000
Stage of Investment: Venture, develop-
                       ment, MBO, LBO
Contact: Philip Wilson

**ALAN PATRICOF ASSOCIATES
LTD (APA)**
24 Upper Brook Street,
London W1Y 1PD
Telephone: 071-872 6300
Fax: 071-629 9035

Minimum Investment: None
Stage of Investment: Start-up, expansion,
                       turnaround, MBO, MBI
Contact: Ronald Cohen

ALTA BERKELEY ASSOCIATES
9/10 Savile Row,
London W1X 1AF
Telephone: 071-734 4884
Fax: 071-734 6711

Minimum Investment: £100,000
Stage of Investment: Start-up, early stage,
                       development, buy-out
Contact: Bryan Wood

**BARCLAYS DEVELOPMENT CAPITAL
LIMITED**
Pickfords Wharf, Clink Street,
London SE1 9DG
Telephone: 071-407 2389
Fax: 071-407 3362

Minimum Investment: £150,000
Stage of Investment: Some expansion capital
                       but mainly buy-outs
Contact: Michael Cumming

BARCLAYS VENTURE CAPITAL UNIT
Clerkenwell House, 67 Clerkenwell Road,
London EC1R 5BH
Telephone: 071-242 4900
Fax: 071-242 2048

Minimum Investment: £100,000
Stage of Investment: All, but emphasis on
                       development capital
Contact: Mike Vallance

**BARING BROTHERS HAMBRECHT &
QUIST LIMITED**
140 Park Lane,
London W1Y 3AA
Telephone: 071-408 0555
Fax: 071-493 5153

Minimum Investment: None
Stage of Investment: All stages
Contact: Richard Onians

BARING CAPITAL INVESTORS LTD
Suite 9, 140 Park Lane,
London W1Y 3AA
Telephone: 071-408 1282
Fax: 071-493 1368

Minimum Investment: £1m
Stage of Investment: MBO, MBI, LBO
Contact: Paul Griffiths

**BARNES THOMSON MANAGEMENT
SERVICES LTD**
120 Wigmore Street,
London W1H 9FD
Telephone: 071-487 3870
Fax: 071-487 3860

Minimum Investment: £100,000
Stage of Investment: Start-up, expansion,
                       MBO, MBI
Contact: Kenneth R Barnes

BARONSMEAD PLC
Clerkenwell House, 67 Clerkenwell Road,
London EC1R 5BH
Telephone: 071-242 4900
Fax: 071-242 2048

Minimum Investment: £100,000
Stage of Investment: Expansion, acquisition,
                       replacement capital,
                       buy-out and buy-in
Contact: Garry Sharp

BIRMINGHAM TECHNOLOGY (VENTURE CAPITAL) LTD
Aston Science Park, Love Lane,
Aston Triangle,
Birmingham B7 4BJ
Telephone: 021-359 0981
Fax: 021-359 0433

Minimum Investment: £20K
Stage of Investment: Seed, start-up
Contact: Harry A Nicholls

BRITISH TECHNOLOGY GROUP
101 Newington Causeway,
London SE1 6BU
Telephone: 071-403 6666
Fax: 071-403 7586

Minimum Investment: £50,000
Stage of Investment: Seed, start-up,
expansion
Contact: David James

BROWN SHIPLEY DEVELOPMENT CAPITAL LIMITED
Founders Court, Lothbury,
London EC2R 7HE
Telephone: 071-606 9833
Fax: 071-600 2279

Minimum Investment: £750,000
Stage of Investment: Later stage, buy-outs
Contact: David Wills

CAMBRIDGE CAPITAL MANAGE-MENT LTD
13 Station Road,
Cambridge CB1 2JB
Telephone: 0223 312856
Fax: 0223 65704

Minimum Investment: £200,000
Stage of Investment: Expansion, buy-outs,
buy-ins, and excep-
tionally replacement
Contact: Stephen Bloomfield

CANDOVER INVESTMENTS PLC
Cedric House, 8–9 East Harding Street,
London EC4A 3AS
Telephone: 071-583 5090
Fax: 071-583 0717

Minimum Investment: £5m
Stage of Investment: Expansion, MBO, MBI
Contact: C R E Brooke

CAPITAL PARTNERS INTERNATIONAL LTD
250 Kings Road,
London SW3 5UE
Telephone: 071-351 4899
Fax: 071-376 5983

Minimum Investment: £10,000
Stage of Investment: All
Contact: Dr Christoph von
Luttitz, MBA
MCIM

CAPITAL VENTURES LIMITED
Rutherford Way,
Cheltenham, Glos. GL51 9TR
Telephone: 0242 584380
Fax: 0242 226671

Minimum Investment: None
Stage of Investment: All stages
Contact: Richard Collins

CASTLEFORTH FUND MANAGERS LTD
10 Charterhouse Square,
London EC1M 6EH
Telephone: 071-490 4113
Fax: 071-253 5636

Minimum Investment: £250,000
Stage of Investment: All stages
Contact: Donald Workman

CAUSEWAY CAPITAL LIMITED
7 Hanover Square,
London W1R 9HE
Telephone: 071-495 2525
Fax: 071-491 2050

Minimum Investment: £500,000
Stage of Investment: Expansion, MBO, MBI
Contact: Lionel Anthony

**CENTREWAY DEVELOPMENT
CAPITAL LIMITED**
1 Victoria Square,
Birmingham B1 1BD
Telephone: 021-643 3941
Fax: 021-631 3739

Minimum Investment: £150,000
Stage of Investment: Expansion and
                        turnaround
Contact: John Naylor

**CHARTERHOUSE DEVELOPMENT
CAPITAL LIMITED**
7 Ludgate Broadway,
London EC4V 6DX
Telephone: 071-248 4000
Fax: 071-329 4252

Minimum Investment   £250,000
Stage of Investment: Expansion and man-
                        agement buy-outs/
                        buy-ins
Contact: Gordon Bonnyman

CHARTERHOUSE VENTURE FUNDS
10 Hertford Street,
London W1Y 7DX
Telephone: 071-409 3232
Fax: 071-629 2705

Minimum Investment: £300,000
Stage of Investment: All stages
Contact: Dr John Walker

CHARTFIELD & CO LTD
24–26 Baltic Street,
London EC1Y 0TB
Telephone: 071-608 1451
Fax: 071-608 3158

Minimum Investment: −
Stage of Investment: All stages except
                        start-ups
Contact: Nicky Branch

CIN VENTURE MANAGERS LIMITED
Hobart House, Grosvenor Place,
London SW1X 7AD
Telephone: 071-245 6911
Fax: 071-389 7173

Minimum Investment: £250,000
Stage of Investment: Start-up, expansion,
                        MBO, MBI, LBO
Contact: Robin Hall (MD)

CITICORP VENTURE CAPITAL LTD
PO Box 199, Cottons Centre, Hays Lane,
London SE1 2QT
Telephone: 071-234 5678
Fax: 071-234 2784

Minimum Investment: £500,000
Stage of Investment: Expansion, MBO,
                        MBI, LBO
Contact: Michael DC Smith
                        (MD)

**CLOSE INVESTMENT MANAGEMENT
LIMITED**
36 Great St Helen's,
London EC3A 6AP
Telephone: 071-283 2241
Fax: 071-638 5624

Minimum Investment: £300,000
Stage of Investment: Mainly development
                        capital; some early
                        stage
Contact: Nick MacNay

CLYDESDALE BANK EQUITY LIMITED
30 St Vincent Place,
Glasgow G1 2HL
Telephone: 041-248 7070
Fax: 041-223 3724

Minimum Investment: £250,000+
Stage of Investment: −
Contact: Alisdair A Stewart

COUNTY NATWEST VENTURES
135 Bishopsgate,
London EC2M 3UR
Telephone: 071-375 5000
Fax: 071-375 6262

Minimum Investment: £250,000
Stage of Investment: MBO, MBI, rescue,
                        turnaround, share
                        purchase, expansion
                        finance, selective
                        start-ups
Contact: David Shaw (MD)

**CREDITANSTALT DEVELOPMENT
CAPITAL**
29 Gresham Street,
London EC2V 7AH
Telephone: 071-822 2600
Fax: 071-822 2663 or 071-822 2644

Minimum Investment: £350K equity + min
£1m mezzanine
Stage of Investment: Expansion, MBO, MBI,
limited start-up
Contact: James Stewart

DARTINGTON & COMPANY
70 Prince Street,
Bristol BS1 4QD
Telephone: 0272 213206
Fax: 0272 230379

Minimum Investment: £100,000
Stage of Investment: Expansion, MBO,
MBI, LBO
Contact: Sir Aubrey Brocklebank
Bt

DCC VENTURES LIMITED
103 Mount Street,
London W1Y 5HE
Telephone: 071-491 0767
Fax: 071-499 1952

Minimum Investment: £1m
Stage of Investment: Start-up, expansion,
MBO, MBI
Contact: Jim Flavin

**DERBYSHIRE ENTERPRISE BOARD
LIMITED**
95 Sheffield Road,
Chesterfield S41 7JH
Telephone: 0246 207390
Fax: 0246 221080

Minimum Investment: £50,000
Stage of Investment: All
Contact: Alan Moore

DEVELOPMENT CAPITAL GROUP LTD
44 Baker Street,
London W1M 1DH
Telephone: 071-935 2731
Fax: 071-935 9831

Minimum Investment: £200,000
Stage of Investment: All stages except seed
Contact: Tom Glucklich

**THE DONCASTER ENTERPRISE
AGENCY (FINANCE)**
19/21 Hallgate,
Doncaster DN1 3NA
Telephone: 0302 340320
Fax: 0302 344740

Minimum Investment: £10,000
Stage of Investment: Any
Contact: Brian Crangle

DUNEDIN VENTURES LIMITED
(Formerly British Linen Fund Managers)
Dunedin House, 25 Ravelston Terrace,
Edinburgh EH4 3EX
Telephone: 031-315 2500
Fax: 031-332 1234

Minimum Investment: £200,000
Stage of Investment: All stages except seed
Contact: Douglas Anderson

**EAGLE STAR INVESTMENT
MANAGERS LIMITED**
60 St Mary Axe,
London EC3A 8JQ
Telephone: 071-929 1111
Fax: 071-626 1266

Minimum Investment: £500,000
Stage of Investment: Development, expan-
sion, buy-out/buy-in
Contact: Carol Ames

ECI VENTURES
Brettenham House, Lancaster Place,
London WC2E 7EN
Telephone: 071-606 1000
Fax: 071-240 5050

Minimum Investment: £500,000
Stage of Investment: Expansion, buy-outs,
buy-ins
Contact: David Wansbrough

ELECTRA INNVOTEC LIMITED
65 Kingsway,
London WC2B 6QT
Telephone: 071-831 9901
Fax: 071-240 8565

Minimum Investment:£300,000
Stage of Investment: Start-up, expansion
Contact: Peter J Dohrn

ELECTRA KINGSWAY LIMITED
65 Kingsway,
London WC2B 6QT
Telephone: 071-831 6464
Fax: 071-404 5388

Minimum Investment:£2m
Stage of Investment: All stages except seed
Contact: Hugh Mumford

ELECTRA LEISURE LIMITED
65 Kingsway,
London WC2B 6QT
Telephone: 071-831 6464
Fax: 071-404 5388

Minimum Investment:£500,000
Stage of Investment: All stages
Contact: Dr Brian Terry

ENTERPRISE EQUITY (NI) LTD
Bulloch House, Linenhall Street,
Belfast BT2 8PP
Telephone: 0232 242500
Fax: 0232 242487

Minimum Investment:£20,000
Stage of Investment: All stages
Contact: Bob McGowan-Smith

**EUROCONTINENTAL (ADVISERS)
LIMITED**
5th Floor, 30 Coleman Street,
London EC2R 5AE
Telephone: 071-600 1689
Fax: 071-600 1967

Minimum Investment:ECU 500,000
                    (£350,000)
Stage of Investment: Expansion and devel-
                        opment finance, MBO,
                        MBI
Contact: Albert Gabizon

EUROVENTURES UK
(Managed by Octagon Investment
Management Ltd)
Cambridge Science Park, Milton Road,
Cambridge CB4 4WE
Telephone: 0223 423033
Fax: 0223 420941

Minimum Investment:£250,000
Stage of Investment: Expansion, MBO, MBI
Contact: Christopher Rowlands

FLEMING VENTURES LTD
World Trade Centre, International House,
1 St. Katharine's Way,
London E1 9UN
Telephone: 071-480 6211
Fax: 071-481 1156

Minimum Investment:£250,000
Stage of Investment: Later stage (expan-
                        sion), MBO, MBI
Contact: Peter English

**FOREIGN & COLONIAL VENTURES
LTD**
6 Laurence Pountney Hill,
London EC4R 0BL
Telephone: 071-782 9829
Fax: 071-782 9834

Minimum Investment:£500,000
Stage of Investment: Expansion, MBO, MBI
Contact: James Nelson

GARTMORE INVESTMENT LIMITED
Gartmore House, 16/18 Monument Street,
London EC3R 8AJ
Telephone: 071-623 1212
Fax: 071-782 2658

Minimum Investment:£300,000
Stage of Investment: Expansion, MBO, MBI,
                        LBO, replacement
Contact: Michael Walton

GRANVILLE & CO LIMITED
Mint House, 77 Mansell Street,
London E1 8AF
Telephone: 071-488 1212
Fax: 071-481 3911

Minimum Investment:£500,000
Stage of Investment: Expansion, MBO,
                       MBI etc
Contact: Michael Proudlock

GREAT WINCHESTER CAPITAL FUND MANAGERS

21 Great Winchester Street,
London EC2N 2HH
Telephone: 071-588 7575
Fax: 071-638 4239

Minimum Investment:£250,000
Stage of Investment: Expansion, MBO,
                       start-up
Contact: Anthony R Campling

GRESHAM TRUST plc

Barrington House, Gresham Street,
London EC2V 7HE
Telephone: 071-606 6474
Fax: 071-606 3370

Minimum Investment:£250,000
Stage of Investment: Expansion, MBO, MBI
Contact: Tony Diment

GROSVENOR VENTURE MANAGERS LIMITED

Commerce House, 2–6 Bath Road,
Slough SL1 3RZ
Telephone: 0753 811812
Fax: 0753 811813

Minimum Investment:£500,000
Stage of Investment: Expansion, buy-outs
                       and replacement capital
Contact: David Beattie

GUINNESS MAHON DEVELOPMENT CAPITAL LTD

32 St. Mary at Hill,
London EC3P 3AJ
Telephone: 071-623 6222
Fax: 071-623 4313

Minimum Investment:£250,000
Stage of Investment: Expansion, MBO, MBI
Contact: Gordon Power

GYLLENHAMMAR & PARTNERS INTERNATIONAL LTD

Little Tufton House, 3 Dean Trench Street,
London SW1P 3HB
Telephone: 071-222 8151
Fax: 071-222 0893

Minimum Investment:£500,000
Stage of Investment: Expansion, MBO, MBI,
                       LBO, restructuring
Contact: Dr Lars Ahrell

HAMBRO EUROPEAN VENTURES LIMITED

41 Tower Hill,
London EC3N 4HA
Telephone: 071-480 5000
Fax: 071-702 9827

Minimum Investment:£250,000
Stage of Investment: MBO, MBI, refinancing,
                       development
Contact: Gilbert Chalk

HAMBROS ADVANCED TECHNOLOGY TRUST PLC

20–21 Tooks Court, Cursitor Street,
London EC4A 1LB
Telephone: 071-242 9900
Fax: 071-405 2863

Minimum Investment:£50,000
Stage of Investment: Start-up, expansion
Contact: Harry Fitzgibbons

HILL SAMUEL DEVELOPMENT CAPITAL

100 Wood Street,
London EC2P 2AJ
Telephone: 071-628 8011
Fax: 071-588 5281

Minimum Investment:£500,000
Stage of Investment: Expansion, acquisition,
                       MBO, MBI, replace-
                       ment
Contact: Garry Watson

HODGSON MARTIN LIMITED
36 George Street,
Edinburgh EH2 2LE
Telephone: 031-226 7644
Fax: 031-226 7647

Minimum Investment: £100,000
Stage of Investment: Start up, Expansion,
MBO, MBI, LBO
Contact: Allan F Hodgson

3i plc
91 Waterloo Road,
London SE1 8XP
Telephone: 071-928 3131
Fax: 071-928 0058

Minimum Investment: All sizes
Stage of Investment: Seed, start-up, expansion, MBO, MBI, LBO,
cash for shareholders.
Expertise in funding
and advice to businesses
of all sizes from hands-
on early stage support
through all phases of
business growth and
restructuring.

ICI INVESTMENT MANAGEMENT LTD
1 Adam Street,
London WC2N 6AW
Telephone: 071-930 1262
Fax: 071-839 7479

Minimum Investment: £750,000
Stage of Investment: Expansion, buy-out
Contact: Jeremy Coller

**INDUSTRIAL DEVELOPMENT BOARD
FOR N. IRELAND**
IDB House, 64 Chichester Street,
Belfast BT1 4JX
Telephone: 0232 233233
Fax: 0232 231328

Minimum Investment: None
Stage of Investment: All stages
Contact: Charles Harding

**INDUSTRIAL TECHNOLOGY
SECURITIES LIMITED**
1a The Broadway, Market Place,
Chalfont St Peter, Bucks SL9 9DZ
Telephone: 0753 885524
Fax: 0753 882359

Minimum Investment: £150,000
Stage of Investment: Seed, start-up,
expansion
Contact: Jan Berglund

**IVORY & SIME DEVELOPMENT
CAPITAL**
One Charlotte Square,
Edinburgh EH2 4DZ
Telephone: 031-225 1357
Fax: 031-225 2375

Minimum Investment: £350,000
Stage of Investment: Expansion, MBO, MBI,
development, final
round, purchases from
existing shareholders
Contact: Mark Tyndall

JMI ADVISORY SERVICES LIMITED
19 Chiddingstone Street,
London SW6 3TQ
Telephone: 071-736 3960

Minimum Investment: £1,000
Stage of Investment: Seed, start-up
Contact: Richard O'Dell Poulden

**KLEINWORT BENSON DEVELOPMENT
CAPITAL LTD**
PO Box 191, 10 Fenchurch Street,
London EC3M 3LB
Telephone: 071-956 6600
Fax: 071-626 8616

Minimum Investment: £600,000
Stage of Investment: Expansion, MBO, MBI,
LBO, start-ups
exceptionally,
replacement capital.
Contact: Barry Dean

KORDA & COMPANY LIMITED
5th Floor, 18–20 Farringdon Lane,
London EC1R 3AU
Telephone: 071-253 5882
Fax: 071-251 4837

Minimum Investment: None
Stage of Investment: Seed, start-up
Contact: Pierre de Vries

LANCASHIRE ENTERPRISES PLC
Enterprise House, 17 Ribblesdale Place,
Winckley Square,
Preston PR1 3NA
Telephone: 0772 203020
Fax: 0772 204129

Minimum Investment: £50,000
Stage of Investment: All types except seed
                             capital
Contact: Robert Sheffrin

LARPENT NEWTON & CO. LTD
4th Floor, 24/26 Baltic Street,
London EC1Y 0TB
Telephone: 071-251 9111
Fax: 071-251 2609

Minimum Investment: None
Stage of Investment: Start-up and expansion
Contact: Charles Breese

LEGAL & GENERAL VENTURES LTD
Bucklersbury House, 3 Queen Victoria Street,
London EC4N 8EL
Telephone: 071-489 1888
Fax: 071-528 6655

Minimum Investment: £500,000
Stage of Investment: Expansion, MBO, MBI,
                             LBO
Contact: Charles Peal (MD)

LICA DEVELOPMENT CAPITAL LTD
102 Jermyn Street, St. James's,
London SW1Y 6EE
Telephone: 071-839 7707
Fax: 071-839 4363

Minimum Investment: £100,000
Stage of Investment: All stages
Contact: Stephen Hill

**LLOYDS DEVELOPMENT
CAPITAL LTD**
48 Chiswell Street,
London EC1Y 4XX
Telephone: 071-600 3226
(Pre Oct 1990 071-236 4940)
Fax: 071-522 5889
(Pre Oct 1990 071-329 4900)

Minimum Investment: £300,000
Stage of Investment: Development, expan-
                             sion, acquisition,
                             MBO, MBI, LBO,
                             EBO, replacement
Contact: Ron Hollidge (MD)

LONDON WALL INVESTMENTS
25 Copthall Avenue,
London EC2R 7DR
Telephone: 071-638 5362
Fax: 071-374 0263

Minimum Investment: £500,000
Stage of Investment: All stages
Contact: Martin Pritchard

LOTHIAN ENTERPRISE LIMITED
21 Ainslie Place,
Edinburgh EH3 6AJ
Telephone: 031-220 2100
Fax: 031-225 2658

Minimum Investment: LEL £50,000;
                             LEPF £10,000
Stage of Investment: Any
Contact: Kathy Greenwood

MARCH INVESTMENT FUND LIMITED
Telegraphic House, 36–39 Waterfront Quay,
Salford Quays,
Manchester M5 2XW
Telephone: 061-872 3676
Fax: 061-848 0181

Minimum Investment: £100,000–£250,000
                             depending on Fund
Stage of Investment: Expansion, MBO, MBI
Contact: William Hopkins

MERCURY ASSET MANAGEMENT plc
(Venture Capital Division – Mercury
Development Capital)
33 King William Street,
London EC4R 9AS
Telephone: 071-280 2800
Fax: 071-280 2810/2820

Minimum Investment: £500,000
Stage of Investment: Expansion, MBO/MBI
Contact: Richard Llewellyn

MIDLAND MONTAGU VENTURES LTD
10 Lower Thames Street,
London EC3R 6AE
Telephone: 071-260 9911
Fax: 071-220 7265/7312

Minimum Investment: £750,000
Stage of Investment: Mostly buy-outs,
                        buy-ins and expansion
Contact: David Hutchings

MIM DEVELOPMENT CAPITAL LTD
11 Devonshire Square,
London EC2M 4YR
Telephone: 071-626 3434
Fax: 071-220 3748

Minimim Investment: £250,000
Stage of Investment: Expansion, MBO, MBI,
                        LBO etc
Contact: Richard Connell

**MORGAN GRENFELL DEVELOPMENT
CAPITAL LIMITED**
23 Great Winchester Street,
London EC2P 2AX
Telephone: 071-588 4545
Fax: 071-826 6482

Minimum Investment: £500,000
Stage of Investment: Expansion, MBO,
                        MBI, LBO
Contact: Robert Smith

MTI MANAGERS LIMITED
70 St Albans Road,
Watford, Herfordshire WD1 1RP
Telephone: 0923 50244
Fax: 0923 247783

Minimum Investment: £250,000
Stage of Investment: Start-up, expansion,
                        rescue, MBO, MBI
Contact: Dr Paul Castle

MURRAY JOHNSTONE LIMITED
7 West Nile Street,
Glasgow G1 2PX
Telephone: 041-226 3131
Fax: 041-248 5636

Minimum Investment: £200,000
Stage of Investment: Acquisition and
                        expansion, MBO, MBI,
                        LBO
Contact: Iain Tulloch

MYNSHUL VENTURES LIMITED
John Dalton House, 121 Deansgate,
Manchester M3 2AB
Telephone: 061-839 9000
Fax: 061-839 1691

Minimum Investment: £25,000
Stage of Investment: All stages. Early
                        stage preferred
Contact: Iain Campbell

**NATIONAL WESTMINSTER GROWTH
OPTIONS LIMITED**
Level 2, Phase 2, King's Cross House,
200 Pentonville Road,
London N1 9HL
Telephone: 071-239 8000
Fax: 071-239 8900

Minimum Investment: £5K (Seed Capital Loan
                    Scheme) Others—£25K
Stage of Investment: Seed, Start-up, expan-
                        sion, MBO, MBI, LBO
Contact: Robert (Bob) C King,
                        Director, Ext 8553

NEWMARKET VENTURE CAPITAL PLC
14–20 Chiswell Street,
London EC1Y 4TY
Telephone: 071-638 2521
Fax: 071-638 8409

Minimum Investment: £250,000
Stage of Investment: Start-up, early stage,
                        expansion
Contact: Caroline Vaughan

NORTH OF ENGLAND VENTURES
Cheshire House, 18–20 Booth Street,
Manchester M2 4AN
Telephone: 061-236 6600
Fax: 061-236 6650

Minimum Investment: £200,000
Stage of Investment: Start-up, expansion,
                        MBO, MBI, replace-
                        ment, rescue
Contact: Peter J Folkman

NORTHERN VENTURE MANAGERS LIMITED
Northumberland House, Princess Square,
Newcastle upon Tyne NE1 8ER
Telephone: 091-232 7068
Fax: 091-232 4070

Minimum Investment: £25,000
Stage of Investment: All stages
Contact: Tim Levett

NORWICH UNION VENTURE CAPITAL LTD
PO Box 53, Surrey Street,
Norwich NR1 3TE
Telephone: 0603 683803
Fax: 0603 685903

Minimum Investment: £250,000
Stage of Investment: Start-ups (selec-
                        tively), expansion,
                        MBO, MBI
Contact: Geoff Evans

OAKLAND INVESTMENT MANAGEMENT LIMITED
Ramsbury House, High Street,
Hungerford, Berkshire RG17 0LY
Telephone: 04886 84656
Fax: 04886 84924

Minimum Investment: £400,000
Stage of Investment: Expansion, MBO, MBI
Contact: Philip Margesson

OXFORD SEEDCORN CAPITAL LTD
213 Woodstock Road,
Oxford OX2 7AD
Telephone: 0865 53535
Fax: 0865 512976

Minimum Investment: £10,000
Stage of Investment: Seed, start-up and
                        early stage development
Contact: Antony Costley-White

PHILDREW VENTURES
Triton Court, 14 Finsbury Square,
London EC2A 1PD
Telephone: 071-628 6366
Fax: 071-638 2817

Minimum Investment: £0.5m
Stage of Investment: Buy-outs, Buy-ins
                        and expansion capital
Contact: Charles Gonszor

PINE STREET INVESTMENTS LTD
Bowater House West, 68 Knightsbridge,
London SW1X 7LT
Telephone: 071-225 3911
Fax: 071-581 0131

Minimum Investment: £250,000
Stage of Investment: Venture, development
Contact: Nigel Webber

PIPER INVESTMENT MANAGEMENT LTD
Eardley House, 182–184 Campden Hill Road,
London W8 7AS
Telephone: 071-727 3866
Fax: 071-727 8969

Minimum Investment: £100,000
Stage of Investment: All stages
Contact: Christopher Curry

PRELUDE TECHNOLOGY INVESTMENTS LIMITED
280 Science Park, Milton Road,
Cambridge CB4 4WE
Telephone: 0223 423132
Fax: 0223 420869

Minimum Investment: £20,000 (Seed Invest-
                        ment)
Stage of Investment: Seed, start-up, early
                        expansion
Contact: Robert Hook

**PRUDENTIAL VENTURE
MANAGERS LTD**
Audrey House, Ely Place,
London EC1N 6SN
Telephone: 071-831 7747
Fax: 071-831 9528

Minimum Investment: £500,000
Stage of Investment: Start-up, expansion,
                       MBO, MBI
Contact: Paul Brooks (MD)

QUAYLE MUNRO LIMITED
42 Charlotte Square,
Edinburgh EH2 4HQ
Telephone: 031-226 4421
Fax: 031-225 3391

Minimum Investment: £200,000
Stage of Investment: Start-up, expansion,
                       MBO, LBO
Contact: Ian Q Jones

**NM ROTHSCHILD ASSET
MANAGEMENT LIMITED**
Five Arrows House, St Swithin's Lane,
London EC4N 8NR
Telephone: 071-280 5000
Fax: 071-623 6261

Minimum Investment: $0.5m (or less, for
                       seed finance)
Stage of Investment: Any, but particularly
                       seed and early stage
                       financing
Contact: Jeremy Curnock Cook

ROTHSCHILD VENTURES LIMITED
New Court, St. Swithin's Lane,
London EC4P 4DU
Telephone: 071-280 5481
Fax: 071-283 0242

Minimum Investment: £200,000
Stage of Investment: Secondary share
                       purchase, early stage
                       development capital
Contact: Jeremy Dawson

SCHRODER VENTURES
20 Southampton Street,
London WC2E 7QG
Telephone: 071-632 1000
Fax: 071-240 5072/071-497 2174

Minimum Investment: £500,000
Stage of Investment: All
Contact: Jon Moulton

**SCIMITAR DEVELOPMENT
CAPITAL LIMITED**
Osprey House, 78 Wigmore Street,
London W1H 9DQ
Telephone: 071-487 5914
Fax: 071-487 5048

Minimum Investment: £300,000
Stage of Investment: Expansion, buy-outs,
                       buy-ins, acquisitions
Contact: Richard A Arthur

SCOTTISH DEVELOPMENT AGENCY
120 Bothwell Street,
Glasgow G2 7JP, Scotland
Telephone: 041-248 2700
Fax: 041-204 3648

Minimum Investment: £50,000
Stage of Investment: All stages available
Contact: Donald Patience
                       (Director)

**SECURITY PACIFIC HOARE GOVETT
EQUITY VENTURES LIMITED**
4 Broadgate,
London EC2M 7LE
Telephone: 071-374 1798
Fax: 071-374 4399

Minimum Investment: £0.5m
Stage of Investment: Expansion,
                       MBO, MBI,
                       development capital
Contact: A E B Wiegman (MD)

**SECURITY PACIFIC VENTURE
CAPITAL**
130 Jermyn Street,
London SW1Y 4UJ
Telephone: 071-925 2395
Fax: 071-930 2348

Minimum Investment: None
Stage of Investment: Start-up, expansion,
                       buy-out
Contact: Dmitry Bosky

SEED CAPITAL LTD
Boston Road,
Henley on Thames RG9 1DY
Telephone: 0491 579999
Fax: 0491 579825

Minimum Investment:£5,000
Stage of Investment: Seed
Contact: Lucius Clay

SUMIT EQUITY VENTURES LIMITED
4th Floor, Edmund House, 12 Newhall Street,
Birmingham B3 3ER
Telephone: 021-200 2244
Fax: 021-233 4628

Minimum Investment:£500,000 (BRPF
                       £15,000–£50,000)
Stage of Investment: MBO, MBI
Contact: John Kerr

**SUN LIFE INVESTMENT
MANAGEMENT SERVICES LTD**
107 Cheapside,
London EC2V 6DU
Telephone: 071-606 7788
Fax: 071-600 3051

Minimum Investment:£250,000
Stage of Investment: Preference for devel-
                       opment expansion,
                       MBO, MBI, acquisition
                       and replacement
                       finance
Contact: David Bays

TAYSIDE ENTERPRISE BOARD LTD
Fulton Road, Wester Gourdie,
Dundee DD2 4SW
Telephone: 0382 621030
Fax: 0382 621014

Minimum Investment:£25,000
Stage of Investment: Seed, start-up, expan-
                       sion, MBO, MBI
Contact: Ian T Long

**THE ST. JAMES'S VENTURE
CAPITAL FUND LIMITED**
15 St James's Place,
London SW1A 1NW
Telephone: 071-431 4381
Fax: 071-431 2531

Minimum Investment:£250,000
Stage of Investment: Seed, start-up,
                       expansion
Contact: Simon Hochhauser

THOMPSON CLIVE & PARTNERS LTD
24 Old Bond Street,
London W1X 3DA
Telephone: 071-491 4809
Fax: 071-493 9172

Minimum Investment:None
Stage of Investment: All stages
Contact: Nat Hone

TRANSATLANTIC CAPITAL LTD
33 Harley House, Marylebone Road,
London NW1 5HF
Telephone: 071-224 1193
Fax: 071-224 1563

Minimum Investment:£25,000
Stage of Investment: Expansion, develop-
                       ment
Contact: Gordon Dean

**ULSTER DEVELOPMENT
CAPITAL LIMITED**
1 Arthur Street,
Belfast BT1 4GA
Telephone: 0232 246765
Fax: 0232 232982

Minimum Investment:£50,000
Stage of Investment: Expansion, MBO, MBI
Contact: Edmund Johnston

VENTURE FOUNDERS LIMITED
West Court, Salamander Quay, Harefield,
Uxbridge, Middlesex UB9 6N
Telephone: 0895 824015
Fax: 0895 823099

Minimum Investment:£100,000
Stage of Investment: Start-up, expansion,
                       MBI
Contact: Joe M Frye

VENTURE LINK INVESTORS LIMITED
Tectonic Place, Holyport Road,
Maidenhead, Berks SL6 2YG
Telephone: 0628 771050
Fax: 0628 770392

Minimum Investment:£200,000
Stage of Investment: Seed, start-up, early
                        stage
Contact: John V Hatch

**EM WARBURG, PINCUS & CO
INTERNATIONAL LTD**
20 St James's Street,
London SW1A 1ES
Telephone: 071-321 0129
Fax: 071-321 0881

Minimum Investment:£5m
Stage of Investment: Preference for 'special
                        situations' (buy-outs,
                        buy-ins, recapital-
                        isations, etc) and
                        expansion stage venture
                        financings
Contact: A Michael Hoffman
                        (MD)

WELSH DEVELOPMENT AGENCY
Pearl House, Greyfriars Road,
Cardiff CF1 3XX
Telephone: 0222 222666
Fax: 0222,223243

Minimum Investment:None
Stage of Investment: All stages considered
Contact: Keith Williams

**WEST MIDLANDS ENTERPRISE
BOARD LIMITED**
Wellington House, 31–34 Waterloo Street,
Birmingham B2 5TJ
Telephone: 021-236 8855
Fax: 021-233 3942

Minimum Investment:£100,000
Stage of Investment: Larger start-ups,
                        expansions, MBO, MBI
Contact: Peter Collings

**YORKSHIRE BANK DEVELOPMENT
CAPITAL LIMITED**
4 Park Cross Street,
Leeds LS1 2QL
Telephone: 0532 442848
Fax: 0532 340959

Minimum Investment:£250,000
Stage of Investment: MBO, MBI, expansion,
                        acquisition, share
                        purchase
Contact: George Shiels

YORKSHIRE ENTERPRISE LIMITED
Elizabeth House, 9–17 Queen Street,
Leeds LS1 2TW
Telephone: 0532 420505
Fax: 0532 420266

Minimum Investment:£50,000
Stage of Investment: Seed, start-up, expan-
                        sion, MBO, MBI,
                        reconstructions
Contact   Donald Law (MD)

YORKSHIRE VENTURE CAPITAL LTD
Don Valley House, Savile Street East,
Sheffield S4 7UQ
Telephone: 0742 722272
Fax: 0742 725718

Minimum Investment:£200,000
Stage of Investment: Development, MBO,
                        MBI
Contact: Paul Gilmartin

The author would like to thank the British Venture Capital Association for granting the permission to reproduce the above material which appears in the BVCA 1991 Directory.

Index